SAYING
YES
TO GOD

BARBARA LACHANCE
with Derek Holser

Reflections on *Saying Yes to God*

"Warning: Don't do what I did and start reading this book at night or else you won't sleep that night! *Saying Yes to God* brings to life some of the most profound and important teachings of scripture with such simplicity that I plan on reading this to my seven and eight-year-old daughters. It's easy for us Christians to say we believe what the Bible is saying but it really never gets integrated into our lives. Barbara's personal stories and down to earth writing style guarantees that you will see how this integration really happens, laughing and crying all the way! As biblical truths came alive for her, they will come alive for you."

- Tom Ruotolo, Founder/Director, Power and Love

"It is rare to discover a true story so beautiful that telling it to others causes you to get choked up. Besides the story of the life of Jesus Christ, I can think of four or five true stories that have affected me in exactly this way. One of those is the story of Gerry and Barbara Lachance. As it reflects their story, *Saying Yes to God* overflows with powerful lessons of love and forgiveness that God unleashed through their lives. You will laugh, you will cry, but most importantly you will learn life-changing truths in these pages."

- Josh Peters, PhD Candidate, Theological Studies, Regent University
Adjunct Professor: Regent University

"Barbara Lachance's autobiographical account of her extraordinary life and involvement with adopting and taking care of children with severe disabilities is extraordinary. Her words so vividly demonstrate how God has used these experiences to shape every aspect of her worldview and faith. The grace, wisdom, and simple elegance that we discovered in these pages rolled over us with each passing chapter like a soft and growing New England breeze that whispers of autumn's leaves turning, seasons changing, and all those wondrous things that have been gathered, learned, and cherished in the harvesting process by a willing soul given over to God's ever expanding fields. By simply saying "yes" and following His voice no matter where it might lead and watching His hand working sometimes quickly; sometimes slowly, but always intentionally, Barbara shares all the emotion, pain, and joy of her and her family's most remarkable journey.

Tiffany and I have a special place on our master bookshelf reserved for well-worn volumes that we return to often as we traverse our own life's path. Whenever we become dry, parched, and in need of spiritual refreshing, our thirsty souls return to these familiar pages and stories to drink deep from again and again, to remind ourselves of all those things that are most excellent, most valuable, and most worth fighting for in life. This small but singularly remarkable book is now one of them."

- Douglas and Tiffany Lively, founders, InVicta Entertainment

"What would your life be like if you gave God an unqualified 'Yes'? What if God were clearly asking you to volunteer as a Teacher's Aide in the Special Ed. Department, would you do it? Probably, or at least maybe. But what if more were at stake – and you were asked to provide a home, YOUR home, as a place for disabled persons to live? That would take some thought. Yet if you did say 'Yes', how would God respond? Would God reward you with good health or carefree days? Perhaps not. But since God always writes Thank-You notes, He more than likely will fill your life with an almost indescribable joy that you can read about in the pages of Barbara Lachance's book.

Saying Yes to God offers a wonderfully exciting challenge as the author inspires the reader to ask: How might MY life be blessed were I to say a radical "Yes' to God?

- Rev. Ruth Merriam, Pastor
Church on the Cape, Cape Porpoise, Maine

"While reading Barbara Lachance's book, *Saying Yes to God,* I was reminded of the words of the Apostle Paul in I Thessalonians 2:7,8 (NIV): "Just as a nursing mother cares for her children, so we cared for you. Because we loved you so much, we were delighted to share with you not only the gospel of God but our lives as well." Paul's ancient words of compassion for a less than functional Church have always challenged me. I believe Barbara Lachance's contemporary story of family community with those some would consider dysfunctional will inspire you in the same way. Along with Paul, Barbara and her family tell us, "the Good News of Jesus not only changes the way we live; it changes the way we love." Jesus came to change the word, but He came because He cared. For those who read it, be they friends, family or future generations, *Saying Yes to God* demonstrates that caring for those we cannot change is an eternal expression of Heaven's love. As a Church leader in New England I have watched Barbara Lachance care for a Church that at times, appeared less than functional. Her caring has led to great change. This is something we are all capable of when we say 'Yes' to God!"

- Bob Hazlette, Evangelist/Prophet, Touch of Fire Ministries

"The greatest equity or resource one can have in the world today is relationships. Relationships are hard work and most people today jump out of them because they don't want to take the time and pay the cost of what it takes to invest (love) in others. But when you jump out, you're not only getting out of the pressure, but also missing out on the promise of being enriched and finding your destiny. Destiny or purpose that comes from God is so big that it requires more than just one to fulfill it. Barbara's story is all about finding destiny through relationships.

Someone once said, 'If you are the smartest person in the room, you are in the wrong room. You need to meet with great people to become great.' I met Barbara 25 years ago. She is relentless in making new connections and when she connects, it's 100%. She is passionate in her relationship with Father God and loves others with the same commitment. For God not only gives us this love, but His purpose is that we become love. The bits and pieces I knew about her impacted me, but as I read her life story, I was challenged to the core. Most people her age would be "settled in" to picking up seashells off the New England beaches and living off of retirement funds. Barbara is bent on giving away her greatest resource, the love of God. She is probably the richest lady I've ever met and because of that, I have been incredibly enriched.

- Pastor Roger Cunningham, International Evangelist/Teacher
Senior Leader LaVina, Santiago, Chile

Saying Yes to God is a page-turner! The term "page-turner" goes back to the time when people read only paper books. And if the story was interesting, exciting, compelling, suspenseful, and fast-moving; it would be hard to put down. You would keep turning pages. You would read it in one or two sittings, and the book would be very gratifying.

Whether your version of *Saying Yes to God* is paper or digital, get ready to read it straight through. It is a "read" that will make you laugh and make you cry. It will help you see love for Jesus Christ and all of God's children tangibly demonstrated in word and deed. This book contains a lifetime of experience and prayerful reflection from a very wise pastor.

I've known Barbara Lachance for seventeen years, and she is more like a bishop or an apostle. Then again, with her Roman Catholic background, we will joke and call her "Mother Superior." Titles and offices can't contain her. She loves the Lord. The Lord loves her, and often speaks through her.

I pray every reader who reads this book will hear the call of God through Barbara and will say "yes" to God, because once you read this book and say "yes" to the call of God, you will never be the same.

- Rev. Christopher Leighton

"I have known Barbara, Gerry and the Lachance family for a relatively short time. However, I have come to love and appreciate these precious people as though I have known them forever. The amazing impact they have had on my family has been profound. As I read this book, I realized that the pages were simply filled with the simplicity of who they have become in Christ. I have been a witness and a recipient of the kindness and beauty of the values expounded herein.

Saying Yes to God will take you through a great journey lived by a great people. The insights are deep and practical jewels to be used in one's own Pilgrim's Progress. I love this story, I love this book and I love the thought of it being read by a new generation who would dare to love and live like Jesus did. Here is the challenge: *Say Yes to God* so you may become and begin your own Revival."

- JC Alzamora, International Prophetic Evangelist

Dedication

I dedicate *Saying Yes to God* to my husband Gerry, who has loved me as Christ loved the church.

To my children: Paul, Christine, Tracy, and Philip, who have given me endless reasons to be a proud parent.

Finally, to my daughter Gretchen, who is with Jesus. Gretchen taught me more about unconditional love than any individual on Earth.

- Barbara Lachance

Contents

1

Hearing from God

JUST SAY YES to God. That's my encouragement to you. But I'm not naïve. Trust me, I know it's not always easy to say "yes" to Him. If only we could wake up every morning with a smile. If only every day began with sunlight flooding every window, and a warm cup of coffee already poured. If only we could roll out of bed with plenty of time to read the Bible, or study the fields and the bright blue sky, all while peacefully whispering "thank you" to our Heavenly Father. If only we could pray and listen for God to tell us what to do. Then, we could just say yes to God. With a morning like that, how hard could it be? With a morning like that, anyone would say yes to God.

But every morning isn't that calm and serene. Sometimes, the morning comes after a dreadful night of anguish and tears. Sometimes, the morning comes like a hurricane. You've overslept, the dog just vomited on the floor, the car has a dead battery, and the clothes you were going to wear for the vitally important, potentially life-changing job interview are suddenly smeared with gooey peanut butter from your toddler's flailing hands.

Some mornings, it's a miracle just to make it to work on time. Many mornings, it's a miracle to even acknowledge God. Some days – most days – it's not natural to say "yes" to God. As much as I love my family, and as much as family matters, we don't always get along. We don't always agree. But, in the moments of frustration, or disappointment, it's perhaps even more essential that we say yes to God.

Isn't it true that God is sovereign? Isn't it true that no matter what happens, He's there to carry us through or He's there to pick us up? Whether we see Him or not, He's there, right? Right?

Yes, He is. I'm not writing that He's there to convince myself. I'm writing that He's there to remind us. God is. And He is waiting for us to say yes.

Because I know this to be true, I've found that saying yes to God is the right answer, even if it doesn't make sense. In fact, saying yes to God often doesn't make sense to my natural mind. But saying yes to God isn't about our mind. It's about His will. It's about His Holy Spirit and the life that He wants us to live, which more often than not runs opposite to what our humanity desires.

Pause and think. Do you believe in God? Do you believe that He made you and He loves you? If so, would you agree that saying yes to God is the most necessary thing for us to do? If so, why do we sometimes have a hard time doing it? Or, even more disconcerting, why do we often tell him "no?"

We don't always realize when we say no to God, or yes for that matter. Often, people feel like they can't or don't hear God well enough to give an answer. The truth is, God rarely speaks in an audible voice. He is all around, but He does not intrude. He is omnipresent, but He awaits our invitation to draw near. I have discovered that saying yes to God is often about saying no to myself. I've learned a lot over the past seven decades and I've discovered there's only one way to live freely and fully. Every day, in every way, to the best of my ability, I must say yes to God.

The only way to discover God in all phases of life is by living in surrendered obedience. My prayer is that by reading this book, you'll find a deeper understanding of what it means to say yes to God, and you'll be inspired to say yes to God every day, for the rest of your days.

I'M AN ALL-OUT kind of person. I live life to the full and I rarely look back. I am a relentless optimist. I'm also downright stubborn. I believe there are things worth fighting for, and I'm not afraid to speak my mind.

There are positive aspects to my determined ambition, and there are negative consequences to my persistent drive. I have grown weary. I have become exhausted. I have experienced disenchantment and disillusion when people break promises or I discover their motives were impure and their agenda was twisted and selfish.

I have experienced life-threatening illnesses and life-upsetting storms. But, I have discovered, like St. Peter, that miracles only come when we are in a circumstance that requires the miraculous. And, like St. Peter, I've discovered that walking on water happens during the storm. *Walking on water only happens when I say yes to God.* I've learned to say yes to Him because

He knows best. He made me and He wants good for me, so when I hear Him ask, I do my best to say "yes."

MY PURPOSE IN LIFE is to tell the world that there are seeds of greatness and fantastic destiny planted in everyone. I believe God begins to give us glimpses of His plan during early childhood, and it continues for the rest of our lives. It may be in the form of a familiar feeling, or a coincidence. Maybe it's a singular irresistible passion. I believe all the above are God's way of alerting us to His design in and for our life.

There is a calling for every one, and God's desire is that we all come into relationship with Him. Now, it's up to us to discover His calling, but when we invite Christ into our lives, it opens a door into an incredible world of opportunities. Not just eternity, but life on this earth as well.

I believe that each of us has a life purpose and it is summed up by the following equation: Your Passion + Your Gifts/Talents/Abilities + The People You Reach = Your Life's Purpose. The first indicator is your passion. What stirs you? What could you talk about or learn about for hours without getting bored or fatigued? This is your passion. Pursue it, while sharpening your talents and gifts but without being reckless. Be patient. God is. Listen to Him and trust Him.

We are given the chance to experience His beauty at work in us. He allows us to be creative and do things we never dreamed possible. All it takes is for us to say "yes" to God.

When we say yes to God, we find a new dimension of life. When we say yes to God, we see the miraculous. When we say yes to God, we discover the world in new colors and brighter light. When we say yes to God, we are given the chance to participate in His work everywhere we go.

There is nothing greater than saying yes to God. That's not to say it is easy. Greatness doesn't come cheaply. Sometimes, saying yes to God is the hardest thing to do. As I've discovered, through the ups and downs, the brightest days and the darkest nights, saying yes to God requires faith and patience.

In Hebrews chapter 6, a compelling passage speaks about the challenge of overcoming our humanity and fully relying on God:

God is not unjust; He will not forget your work and the love you have shown Him as you have helped His people and continue to help them. We want each of you to show this same diligence to the very end, so that what you hope for may be fully realized. We do not want you to become lazy, but to imitate those who through faith and patience inherit what has been promised.[1]

As I think about the experiences of my life, I realize that I've been able to enjoy great blessings and endure great challenges because of the faith and patience that allows me to say yes to God. I guess another word for unrealistic optimism is *faith,* and another word for stubbornness is *patience.*

IN A PAGE OR TWO, I'll get to the details of some of my harrowing experiences and holy moments, my frightening doctors' reports and my fantastic miracles. I pray they inspire you to trust God, and know that you too can survive the storm. It all begins by saying yes to Him.

Perhaps you've read this far and are saying, "Barbara, I would love to say yes to God. I would be happy to do whatever He asks. My problem is I can't seem to hear Him!"

I understand. The noise of life and the busyness of each day constantly choke out the opportunity to listen. Even if we do make the time to listen, it doesn't take long for our brain to jump to something we forgot to do. Or the phone rings. Or the toilet clogs. So much interruption. So little inspiration.

I believe routine is important for hearing from God. Even in the Garden of Eden, there was a routine for God to speak to Adam and Eve. God is a God of order, and while I know He is always available, it seems that He really enjoys a morning meeting and an evening get-together.

Genesis 3:8-13 tells the story of God coming to visit Adam and Eve after they sinned. "And they heard the Lord God walking in the garden in the cool of the evening, and Adam and his wife hid themselves from the presence of the Lord God among the trees."

Proverbs 8:17 reads, "I love them that love Me, and those that seek me early will find Me."

PERHAPS THIS ROUTINE has been established by God? Maybe it's written on our hearts to meet him in the morning and the evening. I don't think it means you can't hear from God anytime - day or night - but I wonder about the tradition of morning devotions and bedtime prayers. Maybe there's a reason these times are so commonly used for prayer and reflection.

I find the morning routine very beneficial. I hear God mostly through reading the Bible. Every time I read it, I discover something new. I find that reading and re-reading a passage over time reveals fresh truth or revelation. Every morning, while I'm getting ready for my day, I listen to the Daily Audio Bible. I'm immersed in the Word of God while I make my bed, straighten up, prepare breakfast, etc.

Gerry and I get up at 5 AM every day. He goes downstairs and I stay in the room. I pray during that time. I just remain quiet and listen for God's gentle instruction. Most days there's nothing earth-shattering that happens. Most days, it's just a reminder to love those around me. God encourages me to surrender my will and serve others. Of course, each and every day, He still gives me the choice. And in that moment, I have the privilege of saying "yes" to God.

WHEN I STAY focused on God, He gives me instruction and sometimes, urgent messages that lead to dramatic miracles. The first time I really said "yes" to God was when I came into relationship with Jesus Christ.

It was the mid-1970s and we went on a family vacation to Myrtle Beach, South Carolina. It was a camping trip, which was a sacrificial act on my part. You know, with the tent and propane cook stove. Sleeping on the hard ground. Sweating. Camping is not for me. My idea of camping is staying at the Marriott Long Wharf in Boston. Or, anyplace that has nice beds, air conditioning, and walls that keep mosquitos where they belong, in the woods! We do lots of things we don't like for our families, and for me, that meant camping. Though camping wasn't my idea, God clearly had plans for me during that trip, as I soon discovered.

I was reading a very influential book in my life, *Nine O'Clock in the Morning*, by Father Dennis Bennett, while sitting near a pond with my three children. The kids were fishing and playing, and I was grateful that I had a few moments to relax. Unfortunately, my husband was not relaxing. While we were appreciating nature, he was battling man's fallen nature – more precisely, the sickness that is common to all since Adam and Eve allowed sin into the world. He had a high fever and a sore throat and was trying to nap in our camper.

As I finished reading *Nine O'Clock in the Morning*, I began to pray. I told Jesus, "I really want to be sure of my relationship with you. Please forgive me of my sin. Please come into my heart and save me. Be Lord of my life. Thank you Jesus. Also, please heal my husband, Gerry, of any and all sickness. Amen."

I was in the midst of a real heart change. The first year I came to know Jesus, I wasn't sure of my salvation. I didn't really understand the Scriptures. That first year, I prayed the prayer above almost daily because I was never really certain that Jesus was my Savior.

On that day, in the middle of camping, all my doubt melted away. All of my questioning disappeared after this prayer, because what happened next convinced me that there is a living and breathing God who wants to be a total part of my life.

As the words left my mouth, I opened my eyes. Suddenly, the sun became very white overhead and it appeared to expand in size. Light flooded toward me from both sides of the sun. The sunrays came skipping across the pond as if the Son of God were coming straight into my heart. I knew then, and have ever since, that I have a personal relationship with Jesus.

While this was happening, my son started crying out for help. His piercing screams shattered my mystical moment with God. He had been fishing in a small pond nearby. My heart jumped into my throat at his scream. Fortunately, he was fine, but he had hooked a duck with his fishing line! I ran to him and wrestled with a hooked duck, trying desperately to free the poor animal without falling into the pond!

As water splashed about, and the squawking duck finally broke loose, I could still feel the tangible love of God and the power of the Holy Spirit. After the duck flapped away, and I swiped a few feathers from my clothes, my heartbeat slowed. My son was grinning with a combination of fright and glee. The day had already contained plenty of excitement, but God wasn't done. Just a few minutes later, my husband exited the camper, fully healed!

UPON OUR RETURN from that trip, my dedication to God reached a higher level. I had the passion and the knowledge to be a minister of God's grace. I started a Bible study. I am an assertive person, and I figured that if I knew Jesus, everybody needed to know Jesus.

But, I had to figure out where it would be held. I knew the perfect place for it, but it would have required a little remodeling. While I believed I was saying yes to God to start the Bible study, it didn't hurt that I could use that need to accomplish some renovations I wanted. Gerry had resisted because he didn't want to spend the money, but one day I discovered a "spiritual reason" for the renovation.

For a while, I had wanted to knock out the wall between our kitchen and dining room. As I read Nehemiah 13, I found the answer. I called out to Gerry, "Come look at this verse!"

Nehemiah 13:4-5 tells the story of Eliashib the priest, who prepared a large room that had previously been used for storage, to be used for the temple.

It wasn't hard for me to draw the correlation from that to our Bible study. Our dining room was filled with guitars and amplifiers. We never ate in there, except during the holidays. In essence, it was a storage room, just like the room Eliashib converted to be used for the temple! I told Gerry that we needed to follow the example found in Nehemiah and make use of that room for our Bible study. And what do you know? Gerry agreed.

I was so happy. The first week, I prayed, "God, I said yes to you. And this Bible study is out of obedience to your desire. Please bring in the people so that they will discover the love of Jesus." I felt peace. I was saying yes to God, so He was responsible to work things out. I brought what I had. Some days, it was a lot, some days it was a little.

One day, it was just a can of tuna and a little mayonnaise. For whatever reason, we hadn't gone to the grocery store and I didn't have much in the pantry. As a good host, I always wanted to serve some type of snack during the Bible study. As I scoured the pantry, all I could find was a single can of tuna fish.

Oh dear, I thought. *What am I going to do?*

"Well, God," I whispered, "this is what we have for today. Hopefully, the people aren't coming to eat my food, but to learn your Word."

I opened the can and began to scoop it out. As I spooned the tuna fish into the bowl, it seemed to increase. I turned the can of tuna around in my hand. It looked like a normal can, maybe 5 or 6 ounces of meat. Yet, more continued to come out with every scoop. It was like the can of tuna was bottomless!

That day, I served everyone in the Bible study with a single can of tuna. I could hardly sit still. I was overjoyed, amazed, and awestruck by God's work. We had our own "loaves and fishes" experience, as week after week, God literally multiplied the can of tuna so that everyone who attended was fed. Over the next several years, as I said yes to God, miracles like this were common.

DURING THIS TIME in my life, many people came to our meetings. Many people came to Christ. Many received the Baptism of the Holy Spirit and all learned more of God's Word. All of that was the real purpose and plan of God, but believe it or not, it was the tuna fish that brought some people to the study.

It was an exciting time and I spent many hours with people who wanted to learn more about a real relationship with God. During this time, I began to understand more about the Kingdom of God. In particular, I learned of His deep desire to bring healing to people. I began reading many books on prayer and healing. I began to have a tremendous burden and a strong faith to pray for people to be healed. The truth is the Holy Spirit wants to work in our lives. He wants to work through us to change the world. One of the main ministries of the Holy Spirit is healing – emotionally, spiritually, and physically. Another word for healing is "wholeness." The Holy Spirit desires to make us whole. I think of the word "sozo", which is a Greek word used throughout the New Testament and is translated, "to make well, to restore, or to save."[2] I believe this happens when we receive Christ and the Holy Spirit and I believe this can happen when we gather together to pursue Him. I believe this because I saw it, time and again.

Almost every week, I found myself praying for the miraculous, and seeing it happen. At every turn, I was approached by people in need of healing. As I prayed, I witnessed people freed of addictions, restored in marriage, and physically made whole. It all flowed so easily and freely. The work of the Holy Spirit was dynamic and ever-present.

Little did I know, the day would soon come where I would continue to experience powerful prayer that led to others' healing while failing to experience healing for myself. My illnesses have been with me for several decades. Yes, several decades. They have been devastating and often brought me near death. Yet, despite, or in spite, of my determined prayers for my own healing (the same types of prayers that brought healing for hundreds of others), I have yet to experience the kind of physical wholeness that I know to be a desire of the Holy Spirit. Through my many illnesses, I have learned over and over again that it's not circumstances that determine my response. I learned that it's not feelings that make up my mind. I say yes to God, even when he doesn't say yes to me.

TWO YEARS PASSED, and we went camping once again. This time, we went to Acadia National Park, a beautiful unspoiled section of country that stretches up the rugged coast of Maine. I might have enjoyed this trip, but it rained nonstop, so we abandoned the campground and drove down to New Hampshire to spend some time with my parents. I was looking forward to visiting my parents, because that meant I'd be sleeping in a house!

Speaking of sleeping, I'd be a liar if I told you that saying yes to God made life a bed of roses. Far from it! Even if I did, you wouldn't believe me. Life is not easy, but God will protect us. He also always has more for us. He has more learning, more growing, and more doing for us. Sometimes the more from God brings a great bit more pain. This was one of those "more" moments – well, it started as a moment but it's turned into years.

The first night we were with my parents, I attended a prayer meeting with my mother, who was new in her relationship with Jesus and just as passionate as I was. There were nearly a thousand people there that night, and the presence of the Holy Spirit was tremendous. This was during a great move of the Holy Spirit in America. It was the peak of the charismatic renewal. The Catholic Church was powerfully moved by the work of the Holy Spirit. The power of the Holy Spirit was flowing freely and working miracles across the country.

We had a wonderful time. I was so confident in God's grace and goodness, I felt like I could walk on water. I felt as if nothing could harm me. Yet, less than 12 hours later, I awoke with the worst intestinal pain I've ever felt in my life – and I've given birth three times!

I entered what the Catholic tradition calls, "The Dark Night of the Soul." I'll go into more detail on this in Chapter 8, but I wanted to include a little snapshot in this chapter, so you understand saying yes to God is all encompassing. It's not an "if-I-feel-like-it" or "when-it's-a-sunny-day" affirmation. It's a "no-matter-what-may-come", "even-if-the-world-turns-against-me", never-ending, relentless trust in God Almighty.

Just the day before I was rendered completely incapacitated, I had been in the blissful presence of God with hundreds of other believers. Now, I was racked with pain and felt fear creeping into my heart. Two days later, my fever reached 105 and I went to the hospital, where I remained for the next three weeks. My intestines were tied in knots and I was bleeding internally. The pain was so severe; it nearly knocked me unconscious. I was diagnosed with ulcerative colitis and cirrhosis cholangitis, an incurable liver disease. After an extraordinary period of joy in the Lord and experiencing His healing for many others, I found myself in desperate need of healing for myself.

My hospital stay was miserable. Some nights, I told God, "Either heal me or kill me, just make up your mind. I win either way!"

WHEN I WAS FIRST ADMITTED, I was in an isolation unit because the doctors were unsure of my diagnosis. When my family and friends came to visit, they had to wear a gown, a mask, rubber gloves, the whole sterile "hazmat" outfit. My room was at the end of a hall to give me more privacy. The entire time, I was expecting a miracle. I wrote Bible verses and put them on the wall. I started reading "Foxe's Book of Martyrs, but after a few pages, I threw it across the room. I tossed it as far as I could. That book was full of courageous people, but they all ended up dead. I didn't want to die. I believed I was going to be healed, and I wasn't interested in being a martyr!

Gerry, of course, was my rock. He was with me, by my side, believing with me for healing. He brought in my guitar and when I had the strength, I would strum and worship. In spite of my agony, I praised God. There were a few times when I'm pretty sure I understood what Job meant when he said, "Though He slay me, I will hope in Him." (Job 13:15)

After a few days of my occasional worship interludes, other patients expressed their appreciation. I think my worship brought peace to the atmosphere. I think my worship brought peace into the area. Once, while I was there, my sister came to visit. She had experienced some hard times and could be cantankerous. She sat by my bed and quietly listened to me play worship songs. If I faded or seemed to weaken, she actually asked me to keep playing. It was ministering to her.

Though I was exhausted, I continued to play worship songs and it soothed her spirit.

Gerry's presence and our praise time gave me courage and strength to trust God. As much as I hated the way my body felt, and I wondered when the doctors would determine my condition, and I waited for God's healing, the thing that caused me the most pain was not seeing my children.

Because of my isolation, I could only see them through the hospital room window. Every once in a while, a friendly nurse would let them slip into the room, wrapped in the sterile outfits, with masks and gloves. They could have been wearing a dozen layers of aluminum foil for all I cared. Just to be able to feel their touch, even through the hospital gloves, was the happiest moment of my stay. It is amazing how many things we overlook when we get busy with the day-to-day of living. A hug from a child brings more joy than a week's vacation. A visit from a good friend can bring unspeakable joy to a person who is down.

During this time, I had many conversations with God. I wasn't going anywhere, and I certainly wanted to talk to Him about what was happening and why I wasn't out of the hospital – or why I was even there in the first place!

I had learned early in my Christian walk to pray in all circumstances and, sometimes the most difficult thing, to give thanks in all circumstances. Though I didn't want to be sick, and wouldn't wish it on anyone, this was an opportunity to put into practice what I'd learned. Once again, my stubborn constitution pushed me onward. I made it my duty to praise God. I clenched my fists, gritted my teeth and began to proclaim His goodness. Wouldn't you know it? As I continued to declare how great our God was, it began to feel less like a duty and more like a privilege. My parched lips praised Him, and my soul soared. Though I was bedridden, my spirit was moved as I honored God with my song.

Now, before you begin thinking that I'm some kind of saint, let me clarify. There are plenty of people who can tell you I'm far from a saint, but you don't need to ask anyone. I'll tell you. Of course, I asked the question, "Why?" What human wouldn't? I don't want you to get the wrong impression. Yes, I chose to worship. Yes, I chose to believe in spite of the lack of healing. But, I asked God "Why?" over and over again. I wondered what I might have done to deserve this illness. I racked my brain thinking about bad decisions I'd made, harsh words I'd spoken. I asked forgiveness for every sin I could think of. Yet, no matter how often I cried out "why me God?" I didn't hear an answer.

Saying yes to God sometimes means saying yes to His Word, which tells us,

> "Abraham believed God, and it was credited to him as righteous-ness...against all hope, Abraham believed and so became the father of many nations...without weakening in his faith, he faced the fact that his body was as good as dead...Yet he did not waver through unbelief regarding the promise of God *but was strengthened in his faith and gave glory to God, being fully persuaded that God had power to do what He had promised."* (Romans 4:3, 18-21)

THROUGH IT ALL, I learned that what Abraham did was possible for all of us. I learned that saying I had faith was much different from fully believing. Just as Abraham had absolutely no evidence in his natural body to believe that he would be the father of many nations, he trusted God's Word. It seemed that God was allowing this to happen and I had the free will to accept what was going on or allow myself to fall into a pit of de-spair. I chose to accept that God was still for me, and I found my attitude improving.

I saw God working in me and through me. I knew that if I kept my focus on God, all would be well with my soul. I slowly began to get better. I wish I could say I jumped out of bed like the lame man who was lowered through a roof to Jesus. That wasn't the case. But I did improve. Every day, little by little, I began to grow stronger. Though I was released from the hospital after three agonizing weeks, it was much longer before I was restored to a semblance of full strength.

My first nine months at home were simply spent trying to recover. I was heavily medicated and had no energy. At times, the passion that was my trademark became nonexistent. Turning to the book of Job was a regu-lar habit. Job became my companion through the pain and frustration of not understanding why I remained ill.

My relentless shouting about how great God was had been reduced to a feeble whisper. Had I known the depths of depression and pain that awaited me, I might never have signed up to believe in this whole God thing in the first place. But, saying yes to God covers every part of living, even when it takes you to the edge of dying. I was about to discover that the miraculous comes in the midst of the hellish, and though we can't see it at the time, it truly does all come together for good when we are willing to say yes to God.

2

Family Matters

"GOD WANTS US to care for retarded children," Gerry said in a matter-of-fact tone. In his typically understated fashion, my husband declared one of God's most significant requests for our lives. Little did I know how much that sentence would influence our future and shape our family.

"Ok," I gulped, after a few minutes passed.

Who am I to argue with God? I thought.

So began the next four decades of our lives, caring for many children with severe special needs, and adopting two of them as our very own.

FROM OUR FIRST breath until our last gasp, the family we are born into and the family we build remain an instrumental part of our lives. It is in family that we first learn about the world. It is through family that we discover identity and find our place defined. Family may be good, it may be bad. Some families are dynamic and inspiring. Some families are dangerous and insidious. For me, saying "yes" to God began with the people He chose to be my family. Family begins with choosing to love when things hurt, and choosing to celebrate when envy threatens to tear the closest siblings apart.

No matter the highs and lows. No matter where we go. There is one truth on this earth and in God's Kingdom: Family Matters. And so, I begin where everything is founded and forged. I begin with family.

It's only right that I spend a few pages spotlighting my husband Gerry. He has spent most of his life avoiding the spotlight, selflessly serving our family and countless others. From our early days in communal living, through my many bouts with life-threatening illnesses and their attendant hospital stays, to the launching of Generational Solutions, his life and his life's work have been an unending series of conversations in which he's said "yes" to God.

Saying yes to God is one thing, but continually saying yes to your family, church, and community, at the expense of your own interests takes the kind of faith that transforms mere words into real action.

Being like Christ is something that many people talk about. A few years ago, "What Would Jesus Do" apparel and knick-knacks were everywhere. Lots of people wore "WWJD" bracelets and t-shirts to remind themselves to think about how Jesus lived, and to aspire to truly follow His example. Preachers and teachers of the Bible constantly encourage us to pursue the virtues of living a life of service to others. As Jesus knelt before his disciples and washed their dusty, smelly feet,[3] so we are to put the needs of others before our own. Jesus instructed His disciples:

> Now that I, your Lord and Teacher, have washed your feet, you should also wash one another's feet. I have set an example that you should do as I have done for you. Very truly I tell you, no servant is greater than his master, nor is a messenger greater than the one who sent him. Now that you know these things, you will be blessed if you do them.[4]

No doubt, that's easier said than done. In fact, it's easy to say, but nearly impossible to do. But Gerry does it. Gerry's been doing it since we met fifty-two years ago.

I grew up in East Boston. East Boston is the kind of place where you don't have to ask what people think. They voluntarily give you their opinion and it's usually not positive.

As I've come to realize that Gerry is genuinely as generous as he seems, sometimes the East Boston girl in me thinks:

> *I never knew anyone could be this selfless. He never gets ruffled, he's so even-tempered – I can't believe he's for real!*

Fortunately, Gerry's love has taken almost all the East Boston sharp-tongued, self-doubting cynic out of me. More than five decades of selfless love from the best husband on Earth will do that to a person, even a stubborn, strong-willed woman like me.

My family was a typical lower-income Catholic home, except that we were French-Irish, in a neighborhood that was almost totally Italian. It was a hard life, and I responded with harsh words (like most around me) and a hardened heart. I was the victim of abuse from several older men. I was perpetually overweight. When I was in high school, I weighed over 200 pounds. As I grew older, comments from adults only reinforced the insecurities that kept me from thinking I'd ever have the kind of life God and Gerry have made possible for me.

Even today, when I begin to doubt my abilities, I can hear my mother's voice in my head:

"Don't start anything because you'll never finish it."

ENCOURAGEMENT WAS a foreign concept in my home. I became all the more stubborn as a response. I became stronger and determined to persevere to prove people wrong. Those who know me well know that those personality traits have remained. I don't know how to give up. The development of a thick skin and a firm hand came during those years of ridicule and abuse. It's true that God works all things together for good. If we are patient and persistent, we will see His purpose fulfilled.

After eighteen years in the negative culture of East Boston, I didn't really love anyone, and I certainly didn't love myself; but for some reason, I always loved God.

I loved going to Mass. I vividly remember when I was confirmed at Sacred Heart, a typical Catholic Church in Boston. Like so much of my conflicted childhood, it illustrated the sad state of my family, but reinforced the hand of God in my life.

The weekend after Confirmation, Sister Rosemary sat in front of my class. The room was buzzing with the giddy delight of children. The excitement of Confirmation remained even though it had been seven days earlier. Sister Rosemary went around the room, asking each child, one by one, what he or she received as a confirmation gift. With great pride, the kids with strong Italian Catholic families proudly announced their gift - $50! They all got $50 – every single one of them. I thought every kid in the room was so rich. Except for me.

The year was 1956. In today's dollars, that would be close to $1,000. I couldn't believe it. I hung my head and looked at the small gift I clutched on my lap – two quarters and a red Missal. In case you didn't know, a Missal is a liturgical book that contains all the instructions and Scripture passages for Mass throughout the year. In a room full of children loaded with money, that's all I had.

"Fifty cents," I whispered, when it came my turn to tell the others what I'd gotten for Confirmation. I heard a few snickers from a couple of uppity girls on the other side of the class. I glared toward them without raising my head.

In spite of my embarrassment at my meager gift, God did something in my heart. Plenty of kids would have associated church with the feeling of embarrassment that flooded me in that moment. For some reason, God protected me. Though it hurt deeply to feel poor in a room full of kids with one hundred times more money than I had, I never stopped loving church. I loved God.

Every morning before school, I got up and went to Mass. I was thirteen. The beauty of the church, the poetry and grace of the rituals, and the presence of God all moved my spirit. It was common for me to sense the Holy Spirit and to hear God's voice. I knew it was God's voice because sometimes He told me to do things I didn't want to do.

I remember one day, while walking home from Mass, God told me, "I want you to go apologize to your mother for the way you've been talking to her."

That was definitely God! But, I did it. Though our relationship still had some ups-and-downs over the years, this early understanding of asking for forgiveness and not holding a grudge helped me become a more patient and consistent mother for my own children. As my husband and I parented together, the balance of Gerry's tranquil spirit and my strong will blended into a force that created a unified family dedicated to serving others and serving God.

WHEN I FIRST MET Gerry, I was barely eighteen years old. We were at a college mixer. His relaxed nature put me at ease. His cute smile put me on edge. Gerry definitely caught my attention, but unlike everyone else I'd ever met, he *kept it*. His lack of pretension and his calm assurance were the perfect balance to my insecure striving and my occasional volatility. After our second dance that night, I knew I was going to marry him.

He was a good dancer and he was handsome. I also thought he came from money, which didn't hurt. In our first conversation, he told me he went to BC. Naturally, I thought he was talking about Boston College, which was where all the rich kids went to school. It wasn't until six months later that I learned "BC" meant Bentley College, now named Bentley University, in Waltham, Massachusetts.

Though Gerry's family wasn't what anyone would call wealthy, they were something much more important: *they were healthy.* When we became engaged, they welcomed me with open arms. They celebrated us. They celebrated life and love. Every weekend, we would travel to the farm, where Gerry and his ten siblings would help with chores and then we'd have a big dinner with everyone talking and laughing. It was like I'd stepped into an episode of The Waltons. Coming from an environment of empty, nearly lifeless family interaction, this was a refreshing and welcome change. In my home, the few conversations were usually arguments over which TV show we were going to watch. There was very little discussion of current events, or genuine interest in my thoughts, desires, ambitions or dreams.

I wish my family's reaction to Gerry was half as warm and open as his family's reaction was to me. My mother was dealing with the stress of caring for my father, whose body was diminishing due to Parkinson's disease. She was sensitive to physical ailments and defects. She was focused on the physical and ignored the spiritual. Gerry was born with limited development of his arm and hand. It was determined that it was hereditary, because both of his grandparents were first cousins.

All the women on his mother's side gave birth to one handicapped child. This limitation affected the appearance of his hand/arm. For my mother, this was a defect to be feared, not a difference to be embraced. In time, she apologized for her reaction, but she behaved no differently than many people who still avoid those with disabilities throughout our country everyday.

For Gerry, it was no limitation whatsoever. It never prevented him from attempting and excelling at many things. He learned how to fly a plane, sail a boat, and drive a motorcycle, among other things.

Essentially, Gerry has been able to do anything a person without a disability could do. He has been a role model to many and an example of compassion to all. Perhaps through his own experience of overcoming what many see as a limitation, he developed the tremendous patience and grace that I've watched him give freely to so many over the years.

As I learned through our care for special needs children, and through Gerry's example with Gretchen, our most severely disabled child, there is no limit to the power of compassion and grace. I have seen miracles every year because of the overwhelming power of love.

GRETCHEN. OH, GRETCHEN. Never was there a case as hopeless; never a child so helpless as Gretchen. When she first came to us at the age of 2 1/2, she was so sick and so frail the doctors told us she'd only live for a of couple months. Gretchen was born thirteen weeks premature. She required constant oxygen to save her life, along with other treatments. Unfortunately, the treatments she received caused total blindness, cerebral palsy, seizure disorders, and severe brain damage.

Gretchen also had a shunt installed in her skull for hydrocephalus. The shunt is a valve that provides an outlet for the pressure caused by a build-up of cerebral-spinal fluid that is a consequence of hydrocephalus.

Every complication and condition from which she suffered was severe in its own right. Added together, she suffered from compounding physical breakdowns and multiple disabilities that caused her to require constant supervision and care. Gerry was relentless in his compassion for her. In our group homes, and in our various ministries, Gerry always gravitated to the youngest and the weakest of the children. Gretchen qualified on both counts. She was in our home for just a few days when Gerry told me, "she's staying with us, forever."

Gretchen required total care, which meant care-givers came into our home on a daily basis (except weekends when Gerry and I provided her care). She needed to be fed, bathed, exercised, and have her diaper changed. Most of all, she needed to be loved. Loving was the best therapy of all – it's the only therapy that heals a soul.

She thrived on human contact and it was always reciprocated. People were exhilarated by her love. She was a wonderful child but whenever something went wrong physically – when she felt the limitations of her body – she would react with self-abusive behavior. It took a long time to help her overcome this behavior. Whenever she tried to bite herself or bang her head against the wall, we would pick her up and cuddle her. We would tell her how much we loved her and she would calm down.

But it was more than just telling her we loved her. We constantly reinforced in her that she was fearfully and wonderfully made. We reinforced her uniqueness and greatness and the love God had for her. We affirmed her beauty and spoke words that encouraged her to know that she was loved by God, that she was extraordinary.

Gerry's love for her was transcendent. He used to call me the Queen and he called Gretchen his Princess. The reality is, Gretchen was the Queen. In our home, she became a monarch for life. She ruled the roost.

Gerry carried her everywhere, like a real-life Bob Cratchit with Tiny Tim from *A Christmas Carol*. The way he cared for her made full-grown, burly, flannel-shirt-wearing stoic New England men cry. Every Sunday, we'd walk into church with Gerry carrying Gretchen over his shoulder. Every single one of his suit jackets and sport coats were stained from the drool and mucus that dribbled out of her nose and mouth onto his shoulders and back. It didn't matter to Gerry. He didn't care a bit about his clothes. He cared about Gretchen.

She was a pleasant soul. Unless she was sick, she was full of joy and peace. If Gretchen wasn't feeling well, she would get angry at other people. If we had company over, she was susceptible to overstimulation. Gerry wouldn't say a word, he'd just go sit with her and she would calm down. I mention her in the past tense as she finally went home to be with Jesus on June 12, 2010, which was also our 45th wedding anniversary. What the doctors had predicted would be a life of only a few months lasted a joy-filled and miracle-saturated 27 years.

For Christmas 2011, I painted a portrait of Gretchen as I imagined her in heaven, blind eyes full of sight, wide open in worship and wonder. When I gave it to Gerry, we both wept. For a while, it hung in our living room until one day Gerry asked me to paint it again, with her eyes closed. He knew she no longer was stricken by blindness, but He loved her – and loved remembering her – just as she was, blind eyes, snotty nose, crippled body and magnificent soul. When Gerry said yes to loving Gretchen, he said yes to God, and as always, the beauty outweighed the tragedy by an immeasurable amount.

ONE YEAR, WE SPENT every major holiday except Christmas day in the hospital. I would get so exhausted from traveling and the sleepless nights caring for the kids that my body would inevitably break down and I'd be admitted to the hospital as well.

While I was in the hospital off and on, Gerry continued to manage the home while running his own business. Every morning, he made sure all of our children were taken care of, that everyone in the group home was doing well, and then he would go to work. Then he would drive to the hospital and visit me in the afternoon for several hours. After visiting me, he went home and took care of dinner. When everyone was fed, he drove back to spend the evening hours with me. At the time, we lived in Mystic, Connecticut and it was an hour round trip every time Gerry came to the hospital.

In spite of it all, he *NEVER* complained. He never complained, but one day, after I'd been in the hospital once again, he became upset with me.

"You need to take care of yourself!" he said.

I thought I was taking care of myself and I told him so.

He replied, "No you're not – don't you think it's important to me that you take care of yourself? I chose you! I love you!"

I realized that he cared for me more than I cared for myself. His overwhelming love for me forced him to become forceful. The revelation of this moment transformed my self-perception. By his comment, I understood that he was offended that I didn't take better care of the woman he loved. He was upset that I was not fully appreciating his choice. He chose me. And he was laying down his life for me and I was not respecting his sacrifice.

I have told Gerry many times that whenever this life ends, either I go first or we go together. But, he doesn't get to go first.

I can't imagine life without him. I understand now what St. Paul meant when he wrote, "Husbands love your wives, just as Christ loved the church and gave Himself up for her."[5]

Gerry has truly loved me – and our children – as Christ loved the church. The miracles contained in this book are in part due to his perpetual sacrifice. The legacy we leave behind is built upon his consistent compassion. The family that we've built and that continues to glorify God is only possible because of his continual denial of himself for the benefit of others.

Other chapters in this book will contain stories of our journey together, and Gerry's role in various circumstances and adventures. This portion is dedicated to his Christ-like love and to inspire every man who reads this book. It's possible to love your family as Christ loved the church. I know it's possible because of my husband, Gerry Lachance.

OF COURSE, OUR FAMILY is more than Gerry and Gretchen and me. One of the wonders of our journey has been watching our three biological children interact with and love the special needs children in our group home, as well as Philip, our adopted fifth child, who was born with Down's Syndrome.

I'll share more about Philip in a few paragraphs, but I want to brag about our biological children. When a family has children with special needs, the children without disabilities can grow tired, envious, annoyed, or otherwise frustrated with the constant attention that's required for the special needs child(ren). Sometimes, the stress and emotional toll that it takes on the parents creates a negative relationship for the children without disability. The incessant doctor's visits, the endless illnesses and the extra patience required by everyone can create a barrier for the other children that leads to bitterness in their spirits.

For outsiders, this may be hard to understand. For those who've never had a special needs child, it may seem like the other children in the family are lacking sensitivity. That's not the case – far from it. I've found most children from families with a special needs sibling are very compassionate. But kids are kids, and every child wants Mom and Dad's attention.

My kids were kids too, and though we all had our moments, I'm proud to say that they all have a tremendous capacity to love and a depth of compassion for others that they likely would never have developed if not for our willingness to say "yes" to God when He asked us to take care of the retarded children.

Our youngest daughter, Tracy, bore the brunt of displacement the most. As the baby of the family, before Gretchen came to live with us, she was used to lots of attention and constant affection. Earlier I mentioned that Gerry called me the Queen and Gretchen the Princess. Before Gretchen came, Tracy was the Princess. When Gretchen arrived, Tracy lost her crown. It couldn't have been easy for Tracy. Gretchen's needs were so overwhelming, Tracy got overlooked from time to time.

Given that experience, it would be natural for Tracy to resent Gretchen and even to reject her. But she didn't. Tracy developed a bit of a tough exterior but God gave her a tender heart. She worked through her frustrations – like all of us – one day at a time and today she is a modern-day St. Francis of Assisi. She cares for animals like no one I've ever seen. On our farm today, we have chickens and goats and Matilda the cow, who thinks she's a goat!

It's nothing for Tracy to rise early, feed and exercise them. She is practically a veterinarian. She has nursed animals back to full strength from the brink of death. I'm so proud of Tracy and the woman she's become. I know that she developed her sense of compassion and care from living in a family that cared for those who couldn't care for themselves.

Our oldest son Paul, has become a successful businessman who loves God. He's married with two kids – our wonderful grandchildren – and he continues to be a part of Philip's life. Every summer, he comes and gets Philip and takes him for a week to do "guy stuff."

When Paul was still living at home, he would spend time with Gretchen. Even after Paul was married, he came to be with us while she was in the hospital in a coma. It was the end of her life, and she was in ICU. All of us were emotionally and physically exhausted. Paul sent us home and stayed with Gretchen through the night. Like Tracy, Paul's experience caring for those with special needs, and indeed, embracing them as siblings, forever influenced his perspective and his patience for the less fortunate in the world.

Our middle child, Christine, is very intelligent. When she was only 9 years old, she read four books a week! She was very introspective and thoughtful as a child. To most people, she seemed shy. Around the time that she was in the 5th grade, we brought our first child into our group home. His name was Allen.

Allen had Down's Syndrome, and he was very low functioning. His IQ was only 28, which means he had very little capacity for communication other than noises and grunts and hand gestures. His mental abilities were around that of an 18-month old child. He couldn't really do anything for himself. In fact, it took me nearly ten years just to get him to consistently be able to put on his own socks.

In spite of this, there was something about Allen's innocence and enthusiasm for life that drew Christine out of her shell. They connected and developed a bond that still makes me shake my head in wonder, nearly thirty years later. They became best buddies. His interaction with her, playing on the floor, laughing and rolling around, made Christine much more outgoing. I guess it's true that opposites attract. Right before my eyes, I saw a shy bookworm – who now has a Masters degree in Special Education and a Ph.D. – build an enduring and rewarding friendship with a person whose IQ never eclipsed that of a 3-year-old.

How enduring was that friendship? Let me tell you. Years after they were children playing in the living room, I had to be hospitalized to receive treatment for a life-threatening illness. At this point, it was too much for Gerry to keep the group home running and out of concern for my health and the family's well-being, we decided to close the group home. That meant Allen had nowhere to go. By this time, Christine was out of our house and married. Guess where Allen went on the day we closed the group home? That's right, to live with Christine and her husband.

I am so proud of our children. All of them love Christ and have a sensitivity – not a jealousy – for people with special needs.

NOW, IT'S TIME to tell you about Philip. I saved Philip for last because he's still around. He still lives with Gerry and me, and so I have plenty of material to share about his life and the way he brings everyone around him to life.

Philip was born with Down's Syndrome, but he also had two holes in his heart and severe respiratory problems. The attending cardiologist told Philip's biological parents that there was no need to repair the holes in his heart because he would likely die before puberty. Philip's condition was not good and it only worsened.

Philip left the hospital for a foster home right from birth. For reasons I don't quite understand, and likely never will, Philip's parents didn't want to provide him with care. When Philip was four years old, he came to live with us as an emergency placement. At the time, my husband and I operated a licensed Community Training Home for the Developmentally Disabled.

It's difficult even now, over thirty-three years later, to describe what he looked like. The closest thing I can think of is a human mozzarella ball. He was limp and pale, with no muscle tone and no energy. He couldn't walk. He couldn't talk. He was four years old and he couldn't even sit up without help! He had a constant runny nose and his respiratory system was constantly infected and causing him horrible coughing spells and giving him breathing difficulties.

When he was brought into our home, his only possessions were a little red wagon with a grocery bag full of clothes and toy blocks. No suitcase. It was worse than someone dropping off a pet at a boarding kennel. This was a beautiful little boy, who had a soul and a mind and a heart. The moment he passed through the door, he captured my heart. For me, it was love at first sight.

As I stood there looking at him, tears welled in my eyes. My heart was breaking for him. Like Gerry with Gretchen, I instantly knew we were meant to raise this one as our own. After they dropped off Philip and all the transfer paperwork was completed, I walked to the phone. I called my caseworker and told him, "You'll never get Philip back – he's mine!"

As we nursed him to health with love – lots and lots of love – Philip began to grow. He began to walk. He began to talk. He began to be a part of our family.

When Philip was six years old we discovered quite by accident that his biological mother had passed away. She died of breast cancer. This led us to write to his father and ask that he give up parental rights so we could adopt Philip. We received a letter back immediately. He said he wanted to meet us. Through correspondence, we arranged for him to come for a visit.

He came to our house, which was a huge Victorian home that had once been owned by a prominent political family. It was also the place where we had our group home for the developmentally delayed.

It was old and beautiful, like only those things can be which are crafted with care. They remain strong even when the finish starts to fade. It's the same with our lives. The one drawback was it had no central air conditioning. We had one room with a window A/C unit. It was a humid summer afternoon when Philip's father came to visit, and we met in the small den with the window A/C unit.

The meeting was awkward and the conversation was forced. It felt as though Philip's father wanted to be anywhere else in the world than in that room with us. It didn't bother Philip at all. He kept trying to climb up into his father's lap. Philip's father had a mustache, which fascinated Philip. He kept trying to pull and twirl his father's mustache, which only made Philip more endearing, at least to me. Our tense moment was made tender by the innocence and curiosity of a child.

As we sat and talked, my two older children, Paul and Christine, kept entering and exiting the room. They didn't say anything. They just kept taking turns, first Paul, then Christine, poking their heads in the door for a minute then leaving. Finally, I asked them what they were doing. The look on their faces was one of deep concern.

Paul whispered, "I'm worried. Is Philip's daddy going to let us adopt him?"

The room was still for a moment. We all understood the question and we all hoped for the same answer. For a few seconds that felt like days, no one said a word. Finally, Philip's father looked at Gerry and me and slowly answered.

With a wavering voice and moist but firm eyes, he replied, "I would never take Philip out of this house. Never."

That was the day that Philip finally, fully became our son. That answer from his father matched – almost word for word – what I'd said to the caseworker the day that beautiful little boy was brought into our home with nothing but a paper bag of old clothes and a few ratty toys.

AS PHILIP GREW, he always knew that we were not his biological parents. One morning, as I was sitting at my dressing table, applying mascara, I heard a rustling somewhere in the room behind me. I leaned closer to my lighted mirror, still dabbing at my eyelid with the mascara pen. A movement reflected in the bottom of the mirror confirmed what I suspected when I heard the motion behind me. Philip had entered the room.

We made eye contact over the mascara pen, via the mirror. His round face and wide eyes were matched by his wide smile. As was often the case, his smile made me grin.

"I think I want to go live with my real dad," he abruptly said. "I think maybe he will treat me better than you do."

I didn't get upset about Philip's comment. I knew we treated him wonderfully. After all, we loved him. As far as I was concerned, he was my son. Actually I wondered how he could reason this out, since he was developmentally delayed. I was quickly learning that Philip was a Savant and excelled in many areas of language, sports, music and vocabulary. Because I loved him like he was my own son, my response was measured. I didn't want to unsettle him.

I slid the cap onto the mascara. I pushed my makeup case toward the mirror and switched off the lights ringing my reflection. I turned in my chair and looked at my little boy.

"Ok, Philip," I replied, "I'll try to see if you can have a meeting with him."

As I said the words, "meeting with him" my heart started racing. My stomach gurgled and flip-flopped inside me. Introducing Philip to his father was filled with potential – for good or bad. At the time, Philip didn't recall that he had already met his biological father. The first time had been positive, but there were no guarantees of what might happen if we met again.

When you love children as a caregiver, even if you know they aren't staying long, you become attached. When you give your life for a child that you hope will stay forever, you don't just become attached; you become forged. Your heart becomes eternally bound to the little soul that came from another but now feels completely yours.

Philip didn't remember meeting his father because he was just a little boy when it happened. During that visit, when we asked to adopt Philip, Mr. Jackson (not his real name) told us he was going to move to Texas and start his life over. He was going to take his daughter Lauren, age 4, (2 years younger than Philip) and try to put the past behind him.

MANY YEARS AFTER Philip said he wanted to meet his biological father while I applied my makeup, I decided to try and find him. All I had was a phone number. I stood by the phone for several minutes – maybe longer – thinking of what I would say. My trembling hand finally grabbed the receiver and I slowly and deliberately pressed the buttons on the dial. One by one, the tone of each number rang in my ear. I finished dialing and waited. B-b-b-br-r-r-r-ring! B-b-b-b-r-r-r-r-ring!

"Hello?" a female voice asked on the other end of the line.

I gulped.

"Is Mr. Jackson available?" I asked.

"I'm sorry, you've got the wrong number," the voice replied.

"Sorry, thank you," I said and hung up.

My spirit was filled with momentary relief. Maybe he's not reachable, I thought. Maybe he's just gone and Philip will not ask about him anymore. You know that's not true, I thought. The next thought likely came from the Holy Spirit. You need to find him. For Philip, and for his father. Saying yes to God, when He wants you to try harder, go farther, or do more, is a legitimate struggle. But, saying yes to God in those moments is often the key to unlocking the miraculous. So, I once again said "yes."

I called information (this was long before Google searches replaced phone books) and asked for Mr. Jackson's number. I was given a phone number and something in my heart told me this was it. My spirit sensed that I was about to make contact with Philip's father.

I went through the same routine as with the wrong number. Deep breaths, shaky hands, long pause. I closed my eyes for a moment. Ok, Barbara, let's get it over with.

This time, a young female voice answered. "Hello?"

I worded my statement carefully. "My name is Barbara Lachance and I was looking for a Mr. Jackson who used to live in Connecticut. Would this be the correct number?"

The woman replied, "Yes, this is his daughter, Lauren. Mr. Jackson is my father."

"I'd like to speak to him," I answered. "This is a personal matter regarding Philip."

When I said Philip's name, the tone of the conversation changed from cordial to very cool.

"I'll let him know you called," Lauren said and then everything went quiet. She hung up.

Not two minutes later, my phone rang.

"Hello," I answered.

"Oh, I'm sorry, I meant to call my dad."

It was Lauren. I don't know if she hit redial by accident or what, but something about her voice told me she knew about Philip. I wondered if she knew he was her brother. I wondered what she thought about my call. Clearly, it had rattled her as much as it had unsettled me.

"Oh, ok," I said.

"Goodbye," Lauren said.

FIFTEEN MINUTES LATER, my phone rang. I knew it was Philip's father. I barely got my "hello" out, and he barely replied, "This is Bob, returning your call" before I completely lost it.

I started crying hysterically. Like any good mother, all I could think about was Philip's heart and his desire to meet his father. I babbled on between shuddering breaths and sniffles about how Philip was such a wonderful person and wanted to see him, and how much it would mean to him. Who knows what else I said. Tears splashed onto my wooden desktop beneath the phone as my halting speech poured out the deep yearning of Philip's heart.

"Ok, I'll come," he abruptly said, surprising me into a momentary calm. Then he said something that made me lose it all over again.

"Not a day has gone by that I haven't thought about Philip and not a day has passed that I haven't regretted not keeping him."

I must have been in shock because the rest of the conversation was perfunctory, like I was scheduling a dental appointment. Like most things in life, the anticipation was more intense than the event. It was done. It had been said. My tears dried up again as we determined the best day and time for our visit.

"Thank you," I remember saying.

"Thank you," he replied.

I walked away from the phone with a blend of jubilation and anxiety rolling around inside of me. I was genuinely happy for Philip. I was also completely petrified by what might happen when they met. I wondered if it would go well. I wondered if Philip might experience more pain than joy. So much was unknown. One thing I knew for certain, Philip wasn't worried in the slightest. When I told him that we were going to meet his father, he lit up like the fourth of July.

When we got to church that Sunday, Philip ran up to the pastor, and just about everyone else in church, to tell them that he was going to meet his father. He was beside himself with excitement. I was just beside myself.

TWO MONTHS LATER, Philip's father came for a visit. It was Christmas time, our large Victorian home was dripping in tinsel and lights, and the peaceful atmosphere that comes during the Christmas holidays permeated every room. Philip's father's wife was with him and they brought pictures of Philip's sisters and grandparents. We had a lovely dinner, and spent the evening in pleasant conversation.

As nice as the night was, I was unsettled. All throughout the evening, they kept asking questions about "my expectations." I didn't quite understand but thought that they might think I would want them to spend more time with Philip or send money or who knows what else. Just as the evening was coming to a close the question came up again.

"So Barbara, have your expectations been met?" Mrs. Jackson asked.

As had been the case for the last couple hours, I still didn't understand the point of the question.

I wanted his dad to leave not feeling guilty for abandoning Philip at birth. Of course I realized this wouldn't happen from one visit but it would be a beginning.

So I responded by saying, "Philip is very happy and living a really good life here with our family. I want to thank you for giving us the privilege of caring for him all these years. And, I don't want you to leave here feeling guilty. You have given us a gift and we are very appreciative. Can we pray for you?"

His father's eyes welled up in tears and Philip laid hands on his dad and prayed for him. As Philip tenderly prayed for his father, the man who'd not been able to care for him, we all began to cry. The symbolic forgiveness displayed in that moment was overwhelming. For Philip, it was simply praying for his father. It mattered not that his father wasn't around. It mattered not that his father, for all intents and purposes, abandoned him. Philip loved his father and it was only natural that he pray and bless his father. It was a special evening. The presence of the Holy Spirit was so real in that moment I wouldn't be surprised if there were hundreds of angels rejoicing overhead.

WE MET WITH PHILIP'S FATHER one more time after that Christmas visit. We were going to visit some friends in Texas and I thought I would muster up my courage and give his dad a call and see if we could arrange for a dinner visit. I knew that just seeing his father once wouldn't be sufficient for Philip. His father seemed genuinely happy to hear from us and asked that we come to his house for dinner. I was pleased and Philip was very excited.

When we arrived, it was clear that everyone was uptight, which then caused me to develop anxiety. Philip giddily burst into the large, beautiful home in the Houston suburbs with no hesitation and shouted,

"Daddy! Daddy! I'm here!"

Silence was all Philip and the rest of us heard in reply.

Philip's father was upstairs and didn't come down for at least 20 minutes. We sat with Philip's uncle, his sister and her fiancée, an aunt and uncle and Mr. Jackson's third wife all the while waiting for him to come down. Philip was so happy to be there, he was completely oblivious to our tension. He didn't notice our apprehensive chatter and the awkwardness of us trying to make small talk with the complete strangers who felt as odd about the situation as we did.

Finally, Philip's father came down and Philip got to see him. Philip was thrilled. Eventually, things felt a little less awkward. Philip can put the most hardened person at ease. His gentle, friendly manner can outlast any tension. Everyone loves Philip. But this evening was different and very strained. Nobody paid attention to Philip and again he was oblivious to what was happening, thank God. After dinner we visited for a while and finally it came time to leave. Philip's dad asked him to give him a hug. That was the last time we saw or heard from him.

I came away very sad, not so much for Philip, but for his family. They had missed out on so much by not trying to understand the beauty and uniqueness of Philip's life. Their loss was our gain but my heart went out to them and to those who are so interested in their own selfish desires that they can't see the greatness around them.

IT WAS ONE THING TO LOVE Philip and bring him into our family. That was easy. It was another thing entirely to forgive the cardiologist who recommended when Philip was an infant that he not have heart surgery because "Philip will be dead before puberty." It was also another thing entirely to forgive Philip's parents for giving him up at birth.

I know that Jesus told his disciples in Matthew 6:15, "If you do not forgive others their sins, your Father will not forgive your sins." Knowing the Scripture didn't make it any easier. For a while, I went around with bitterness in my own life because I struggled to forgive the people who failed Philip in such a serious and life-endangering way. I carried my own sin of un-forgiveness because I was angry with them for not taking responsibility for his well-being.

But, saying yes to God comes in many different forms. It comes in ways that make sense and in comes in ways that cut to the core of our humanity. Forgiveness is certainly one of those ways in which saying yes to God makes little sense and crushes our flesh.

"Yes I will forgive, yes I will bless his father, and yes I will not allow the anger to fester inside of me" was all part of my saying yes to God.

God changed my heart and it made for a better home for Philip. I learned the more I love those who don't respond the way I want them to, the more I am at peace. And that is good for everyone, not just me.

Today, Philip is a man of God. He's a prayer warrior. He makes friends everywhere he goes. He has a job at a local restaurant, and he is the toast of the town. He travels with me, and, of course, I'm introduced not as Barbara Lachance, but as "Philip's mother."

One of my favorite stories about Philip occurred during one of his visits to his older brother Paul's house. Paul played in a men's hockey league, and Philip loved going to the games and cheering on his big brother. Years after he entered our house in his little red wagon with snot running everywhere and unable to speak, Philip sat in the stands, screaming at the top of his lungs, jumping up and down, cheering on his big brother.

After the game, Philip got to join the team in the locker room. All the big burly hockey players were chatting loudly, some a little more boisterously than others. Some were using colorful language – a little too colorful for Philip. Paul still laughs today when we talk about what happened next. Bold, confident Philip stood up and interrupted the noise with a loud declaration to all the strong, athletic hockey players.

"Guys!" he yelled, "You shouldn't say those words. My mom wouldn't like you talking like that!"

The hockey players looked at Paul quizzically, and some started to laugh. But, since that day, whenever Philip visits the hockey team, no one uses any profanity.

That's my Philip. That's my family - bold, caring, and exceptional. The Father's heart of God is a wonderful thing. As good as it gets with family, we can't ever out-do His heart. I feel like a spoiled child with a Father who wants to give his daughter the most wonderful gifts imaginable.

At times, I feel like Lil' Orphan Annie, as Daddy Warbucks showered her with presents. Only it's much greater than any material possession. The love of our Father is absolutely transcendent. Has it been easy? Ha! Not a chance. Has it been simple? Hardly! But, it's been the best life – better than I could have imagined – all because long ago, I decided to say "yes" to God.

3

The Next Generation

ANGELA Merkel, Chancellor of Germany and de facto leader of the European Union, grew up in Communist-controlled East Germany. Her father was a pastor with the Lutheran Church, one of the few churches to continue to serve both East and West Germany during and after the separation of the country. In 1954, the year he took his family from Berlin to East Germany, almost two hundred thousand East Germans traveled in the opposite direction.

The church asked him to move again a few years later. Remaining in East Germany, this time Angela's father led his family to the village of Templin in 1957, an area surrounded by forests and lakes. The parsonage was located on the grounds of the Waldhof, a compound of homes and workshops run by the Lutheran Church. A large portion of the Waldhof was dedicated to provide housing and job training and employment for the mentally disabled.[6]

From the age of three until she went off to college, Angela lived among many mentally handicapped people. In an article published in the New Yorker magazine, Angela remarked on the effect of this upbringing as it influenced her approach to people – "To grow up in a neighborhood of handicapped people was an important experience for me. I learned back then to treat them in a very normal way."[7]

Merkel is known for her strength and her calm demeanor. She is described in another article for possessing humility and approachability.

"She lives modestly and doesn't look down on her colleagues in Europe, nor fellow citizens in Germany. And yet – and in part because of those qualities – she's emerged as the one figure uniquely suited to deal with two of the biggest crises facing the West today."[8]

I find it more than coincidental that a woman considered by many to be the most powerful lady in the world has a heart of understanding and humility that was shaped by her childhood familiarity with those in our society who are most often ostracized or neglected. In our era of genetically designed babies, and abortion of babies with birth defects, many Americans live their entire life without any meaningful exposure to the mentally disabled.

Our family was the opposite. The experience my natural children had with the children in our group home, and with their adopted siblings did more than make an impression on their life, it influenced every aspect of their relationships with people from all walks of life.

As I discussed writing this book with my children, they began sharing their own memories and insights. Not just about life with mentally disabled siblings, but life in the Lachance household. As a person with less life remaining than what has already passed, I found our conversations were rich with meaning and, in many ways, encouraged my soul. I think every parent and grandparent, when the dust is settled, longs for nothing so much as the love, respect, and affection that – God be praised – still remains between my grown children and me.

I asked them if they would share their unique perspective of life in a family that was/is unique by any measure. They were eager to do so, and I am grateful for their addition to this book. What follows are their thoughts, in their own words. If you're a parent, I hope it encourages you to raise your children to be the best they can be. If you're a son or daughter still living at home, I hope it inspires you to be the best son or daughter you can be.

Christine Lachance Carver: Lessons Learned from My Mom & Dad

THERE isn't one single event that characterizes or summarizes the lessons I've learned from my parents. When I reflect on our lives, it comes to me like a series of vignettes. My memories flash through my mind like one of those ensemble cast movies that shows a three to five minute glimpse of a few characters, and then jumps to another part of the story. Unlike those movies, my life was very real, and the lessons I learned transcend formulaic humor or drama.

I certainly don't think anyone would describe my childhood as typical and certainly not normal; at least not in the way society defines the word.

Society, however, isn't always right. In my case, the values and principles that my parents instilled in me, which I still carry today, have helped me immeasurably.

One of the most important values that I learned from my parents was that **All People Have Value.**

This began during the years that we were in the Catholic Church, but it extended throughout my life. As my parents worked within the church, and with people who had disabilities, I observed and embraced the notion that everyone should be treated with equal hospitality and compassion. The remarkable thing about Mom and Dad was that you could never tell by their behavior whether a person visiting us was a pauper or a prime minister. They treated everyone the same – with dignity and respect.

It was typical to have a varied and unique group of guests during dinner time at our house. We'd have friends, politicians, family, and church leaders, alongside the physically disabled and the mentally handicapped. I never knew who was going to live with us or why they were there. It did not seem to matter. All I knew was that people needed help and my parents provided the support and care that was needed for however long the people needed it.

Mom and Dad's decision to open the group home, and even more, their adoption of Philip and Gretchen, was a testament to their values. I am sure that most people would have thought that adopting Philip and Gretchen would be a lifelong burden, yet my parents never hesitated to help children in need. I vividly remember every Sunday, while others sat in the back of the church, my parents, along with the residents from the mentally retarded group home, would march to the front of the church and sit in the front pew. Mom and Dad were bringing God's children into His presence, and like God, they were never ashamed, and never hid those they cared for from the rest of the world.

The truth is, my parents are very rare people in that they honestly don't think of the disabled any differently from the way they think of everyone else in society. Sometimes, this led to some very unusual people entering our home. I have certainly seen some interesting, even strange, people in my life because my parents loved everyone equally.

Another important value that was instilled in me was that **Life is About Serving Others.**

When I was a child, my parents gave up their possessions and served the church. They owned nothing, and cared for others constantly. To me, it was just our life, but now I realize how rare that kind of life is. I learned that you should always help others. Time after time, I watched my parents open their doors and serve others. When we moved to Wauregan, Connecticut, they worked with a ministry team called Ave Maria House, which blessed all sorts of people, from all walks of life, who all had one thing in common: desperate and isolating need. Whether it was physical or spiritual, my parents faithfully gave of themselves to meet the needs of those around them.

We moved to Norwich when I was in the sixth grade. I was 11 years old, and we were in a new city, with new opportunities. I had new interests – I loved reading, especially books by Christian authors. We weren't there long when Mom and Dad began serving in God's Gift House. This was actually before they started serving in Ave Maria House. When all you've ever seen is your parents serving, the order of events gets muddled. For some children, a parent serving the needy during a holiday or at a special event is memorable. For me, if there was ever a day that my parents weren't serving, that would have been memorable.

God's Gift House was a prayer community for the handicapped. We had all kinds of people live with us. It was normal for us to play with people with mental disabilities. My parents worked with handicapped individuals from all over the Diocese, as well as the many street people who had been released from the Norwich State Hospital, for the mentally ill.

I remember frequently going with them to the local soup kitchen, where we children helped right alongside our parents, handing out meals, saying a prayer and extending compassion to the hungry and homeless. No matter where we lived, no matter what we did, our family served others. That virtue remains with me today, and the most amazing thing is that it remains with my parents. Even as they are both now over 70 years old, they continue to care for people in need. They never stop serving others.

I could probably write a book of my own on the values that I learned from my parents, but I'll conclude my thoughts for this book with one last principle. I think the reputation of New Englanders as hard-working, no-nonsense people is still intact. Even if that reputation has faded over time, it's as strong as ever in my home. My parents taught me that **Diligence and Attitude Make Anything Possible.**

When I was sixteen years old, my dad drove me to my first job. I was very excited, also nervous, as I started working as a clerk at The Corner Cupboard, a health food store. I learned many things during those early days working, but most of all I learned to work hard. Diligence may perpetually be in short supply, but I learned it was my key to success. My parents expected all of us kids to work hard in school and to go to college.

College – that notorious time of indecision and the young person's search to "find herself." It's a puzzling time isn't it? For me, the season of searching included several changed majors, and a brief pursuit of a marketing degree at Bentley College. That lasted a year before I decided to go to Southern University. Six months after attending Southern, I decided to move home.

I'll never forget when I called my mother to tell her. I knew she would react with great excitement because I believed that God told me to move back home. I was home on break, and we were standing in the kitchen. Soup was simmering on the stove and Mom had her back to me, as she sliced fresh bread.

"Mom," I said, as I stood up from the small table in the corner of the kitchen.

"Yes," she replied over her shoulder, still busily cutting slices of bread.

"I want to come home from Southern."

Mom paused, knife just above the golden brown loaf. She turned and looked at me, her eyes as full of life as ever. (Even when hospitalized, Mom's eyes dance, expressing the power of a soul untouched by physical hardships.)

"What are you talking about?" she finally asked.

I paused. I knew the answer, because I knew how Mom would respond. You see, during that "finding herself" period I mentioned, I had not been active in my faith. I know Mom had been praying daily for me, and I knew what I was about to say would bring a shout of joy.

"Don't get all excited," I said.

"Just tell me," Mom pushed.

"I think it's because God wants me to. He told me to." I let the words sit in the air for a minute. Mom did as well.

The next couple sentences are from Barbara, as she recalled that moment in the kitchen:

I am interrupting Christine's story, because every praying parent knows that what can be a simple declaration in the mind of your child may be the answer to years of prayer in your heart. When Christine said that "God told her to come home", I patted my heart and told it to be still. She was saying yes to God, and I was relieved and rejoicing (on the inside).

It's not that Christine was a troublemaker or a bad child, but when your son or daughter isn't close to the Lord, it's not easy to trust Him and not be pushy. I share this to encourage all parents. Keep believing for your children. God will bring them home.

Back to Christine's side of the story:

I'm not surprised Mom had to interject. She's a very passionate person, and as I now have children of my own, I understand her love and devotion in ways I never comprehended when I came home from college.

"God said what?" Mom asked.

"God told me to come home," I repeated.

Mom played it cool. "Well, isn't that great, you heard from God," she said.

It was that simple and direct. Mom had heard from God her whole life, so maybe she wasn't too surprised by it. But I was filled with a combination of emotions. The strongest of all was peace. I was coming home, because God told me so.

Later, when Dad came home from work, he and Mom had a joy-filled conversation.

I heard Mom telling him, "You'll never guess what God told Christine!"

I let them be and went off to my room to think about this amazing mystery of hearing from God. And saying "yes" to Him.

Everyone was happy. Especially me. I said "yes" to God, and I came home, still not sure what was next for me. But, God didn't disappoint. He never does.

That Christmas, God confirmed His direction for me to return home. One night, I woke up after having a dream about a guy who had come to Mom and Dad's annual Christmas party. Now, that might not mean much to some people, especially since my parents' Christmas parties are legendary. They have so many people come, it's a madhouse of celebration and joy!

But this felt different. In my dream, a light came down from above, and the guy's whole countenance changed. I couldn't get it out of my mind. I didn't know him, other than the fact that he was in Mom's church.

The next night, I kind of decided to go to church on a whim. Not everyone in the family was going – it was a Sunday night service – because we often relaxed in the evening. To be honest, I can say with a clear conscience that when I decided to go that night, I wasn't thinking about the man in the dream. But, when I walked into the service, I saw him. I didn't know his name, so I asked Pastor Joe his name.

"Kevin. That's him over there," Joe answered, raising his hand to wave.

Don't point at him, I thought to myself. I could feel my face flush ever so slightly.

"Thank you, Joe," I said and quickly found my seat.

Throughout the service, I sat fidgeting and distracted, thinking about my dream. Thinking about Kevin. As the service ended, Kevin went forward for prayer. My heart was racing. But, God was just getting started. The pastor beckoned me over to him after Kevin was finished praying.

"Christine, meet Kevin," he said, "Kevin, meet Christine. Joe turned to me and smiled. He just stared at me grinning while we shook hands.

(Thanks, a bunch for making things more awkward, Pastor!)

As awkward as the moment felt, I'm glad it happened. And I'm sure glad I said "yes" to God when He told me to come home. Kevin and I have been married now for 27 years and I couldn't imagine life without him.

Even when I was unsure about my future, I was never unsure about my place in my parents' hearts, and I was never unsure about remaining diligent. They supported me no matter what. They encouraged me to get advanced degrees and often supported me financially. I have been fortunate enough to earn my Bachelors in Education, and a M.Ed. in Special Education, both from the University of Connecticut. After years of hard work, when I earned my doctorate in Educational Leadership from UCONN, Mom threw a party, which may have been bigger than my wedding! My heart is warmed every time she introduces me as "My daughter, the doctor." In that moment, as I see her pride, I know it was all worth it. I know that hard work pays off because I've seen it in my parents' lives, and now I see it in my own.

Paul Lachance:
My Life as the Oldest Son of Gerry and Barbara Lachance

I HAVE MANY MEMORIES from my experiences with Philip. He and I are 10 years apart. I was 14 years old when he came to our home. As he grew up, the interaction between Philip and my friends was very meaningful for him, as well as for them. I can never forget my friend Scott, who lived across the street from us. He probably never had a relationship with anyone else with mental disabilities. These were the days that not many developmentally challenged kids were in schools. This was during the early 1980's, and mainstreaming children with developmental disabilities was just beginning; it was the beginning of the end of widespread institutionalization of kids like Philip.

Scott and I worked with Philip for hours on end, helping him gain the strength and skill to walk. We would take turns encouraging Philip, back and forth; some days we'd keep him going, most days he'd keep us laughing. I'll never forget the smile on Scott's face when Philip would walk toward him for his reward – a giant hug! Philip knew how to hug and he knew how to smile.

Philip smiled constantly, and it was contagious. Our family had a swimming pool when I was in high school, and it became a popular place for lots of kids. My friends would come over and Philip would be right there – he loved to swim with us. He was still very young, and didn't really understand the concept that you couldn't breathe underwater. We would all jump in the water and he would still have his mouth open, looking at us with a big smile on his face. My friends would always crack up laughing. They loved hanging out with him. As life continued, and I moved away, Philip would still come to visit. My adult friends, some of whom didn't know Philip as children, have the same pleasure and camaraderie that I observed years earlier.

One night during a visit as an adult, we ended up at a honkey-tonk biker bar near where I live. The place was jumping – loud music, dancing – just a lot of people having a great time. Philip, as usual, was the center of attention. He must have danced with every woman in the place. He is a great dancer. Just like in the pool years before, he had that constant smile on his face. Philip has a heart condition, so we had to constantly force him to take a break from dancing so he would not overheat. When we did, we had to drag him off the dance floor!

Another memorable time was when Philip was visiting as an adult and I had a group of musician friends over. We were playing music. Philip sat nearby, enjoying the scene, and smiling. Always smiling. I asked him if he would like to rap for us. My friends had never seen this before. Everyone got quiet and Philip broke it down. He rapped a wonderful, long, rhythmic series of prose that blew the group away. He got the loudest ovation of the night – it was really special, and remains one of my favorite memories.

I'm proud of my parents for bringing Philip into our family and I'm proud of Philip for being himself. The power of his smile and his warm spirit breaks every barrier. He opens people up to understand that in spite of observable differences and limitations, the developmentally delayed are normal people who love to have fun.

LOTS OF ORGANIZATIONS and ministries claim to have "open arms" to people. I don't doubt the intentions, and I know there are some that truly live up to the call to love everyone equally, regardless of social, economic, or cultural background – or physical or mental disability. In my home, it was daily. Over the thousands of meetings I observed between my parents and others as I grew up, I cannot think of a single time when they didn't treat every person with respect and compassion. I have seen them talk with high-ranking political leaders, sports heroes, and homeless people. None were treated differently. All were given honor.

As a result of their example, I see value in all humans. Regardless of color, economic status, or disability; I appreciate people for who they are, not what they have or can do. This important truth has steered me through life. In particular, my understanding that **No One is Disposable** has guided me in most of my interactions with others as an adult.

This message has been very significant in my career. As an adult, I've discovered that **Making Everyone Feel Special** is the cornerstone for my success. Actually, making everyone feel special is my success. I don't care if I'm talking with a vice-president of a major corporation or the janitor at an out-of-the-way strip mall. I believe that we must treat every person with respect. I believe in using clear and appropriate communication. When we do that, and empower people within their limits, it's amazing what can be achieved.

In business, when things go wrong or problems arise (which is a guarantee in life), because I've lived by this principle, I have an ability to "rally the troops". I can communicate clearly, because I've built trust. Everyone is more than willing to pitch in and solve the problem. Everyone works together in a collaborative fashion because I've spent the past years – as my parents taught me – making everyone feel special. My parents taught me that the true measurement of a business partnership is not always in our successes, but also in how we handle problems and failures. Living with the understanding that no one is disposable, and making everyone feel special has led to many great relationships, and lots of unforeseen opportunities.

MY WIFE COMPLETELY SHARES these values. She talks with anyone and everyone and treats all people with great respect. Our relationship is perhaps easier than some because of our shared conviction that every person has dignity and must be treated with the same. My hope is that we instill the same values in our children. As our world becomes ever more globalized, and the Internet brings people together from almost every corner of the planet, I believe these values are an absolute requirement for my children (and grandchildren) to be successful citizens of the future.

I've already been able to see the power of kindness and compassion overcome cultural and language barriers. In 2012, my family and I went on a three month trek through Central America. We visited Nicaragua, Costa Rica, and Belize. We met all kinds of people from all types of social and economic backgrounds.

We traveled on "chicken busses", and visited people in their homes and the local schools. We ate in local restaurants. We really got to know the culture. Again, I learned from my parents. They have traveled all over the world in the same manner. They don't go to the "Americanized" areas, the typical tourist stops. And neither do we.

Which is how I came to meet Norlan and his family. Norlan was a guy bagging our groceries at a small supermarket in Granada, a Spanish-colonial city in central Nicaragua. We had decided to stay there for two weeks – in Granada, not the supermarket – and when it came time to checkout, I went to use my credit card, but didn't have my passport. In order to prevent fraud, the store required me to have my passport to use my credit card.

No one really spoke any English around me. Here I was, trying to get our food and supplies for two weeks, and I had no way to pay. Not to mention, people were standing in line behind this stupid American who couldn't pay!

Through lots of effort and awkward hand signs, and the manager repeating, "No Problema", it was decided that Norlan, the young guy bagging the groceries I couldn't pay for, would take me back to the apartment we had rented to get my passport.

Next thing I know, I'm am on the back of a scooter, zipping through the city, dodging burros and mopeds. Along the way, Norlan was shouting out the importance of historical sites. It was the craziest, most fun tour I'd ever received. When we got to the apartment, my family laughed as I walked up with no groceries, and Norlan. We got my passport, went back and got the groceries, and later that day, spent many hours with Norlan and his family. He was married and had a young son. We practiced our Spanish, and continued to tour the city – this time on foot instead of on the back of his scooter!

There are no barriers when you live this way. These are the kinds of memories and experiences you have when you skip the giant cruise ship. This is the way I was raised, and I am grateful for it.

These realizations have been truly transformative principles in my life, and now in the lives of my children. The power of what my parents instilled in us will continue to bring benefits throughout the generations. Though I'm sure sometimes they were tired and even exhausted, their relentless spirit of hope and help, and their determined belief that no one is disposable, has guided my life, and hopefully, blesses the life of everyone I meet.

Tracy Lachance
Last but Not Least, Loved Beyond Belief:

REMEMBER HOW MOM mentioned that she is stubborn? Yeah, I got that one from her. We have an uncanny ability to connect. You know how they say twins can finish each other's thoughts? Well, Mom and I aren't twins, but we sure do think alike. My brother Philip is paranoid about the weather, because it's one of Dad's main topics of conversation. It's like every day, there's got to be a discussion of what's happening with the weather. Doesn't matter if it's raining or sunny, snowing or blazing hot, Dad will bring it up. And Philip is like a little echo chamber, repeating whatever Dad has said.

So, Mom and I will be in the kitchen and I'll look over at her, across a pot of boiling noodles, or over the island, covered in fruit, flowers and newspapers.

"Hey Ma," I'll say with a grin, "Did ya see the weather this morning?"

She'll look up at me, and just start laughing. We both laugh hysterically, thinking about nearly every morning of our lives, as Dad and Philip will talk in great seriousness about the weather. We will laugh so hard that tears start to fall. Imagine all the endorphins that are released with that kind of deep laughter. Great, right? It's a little thing, but a shared sense of humor is one of the strongest bonding agents in humanity. And we have it. The first thing I think about from my childhood is **Laugh Every Day**.

When I think about it, my parents' joy in all things is damn near miraculous. But that's God in them. And the ability to laugh when things are honestly tough and sometimes downright miserable is a gift from God and made my childhood totally wonderful.

IF YOU CAN'T TELL YET, I've got a bit of a different way about me. I'm a plain talking, straight shooting, get stuff done no matter how hard or how long it takes kind of woman.

I love the outdoors. I love the earth. I sucked at school. I hated it. But, if there's a problem that needs solving, I'm jumping in to help. I am not just standing around talking about how stuff should be done. And if someone shows me how to do something, I can repeat it. I love to work. Except for pulling weeds in the garden. You can have that.

Like I mentioned earlier, Mom and I have some common personality traits. This has given our relationship great depth and also has tested us. Mostly, we just agree to disagree. No matter what, though, if something is bothering me, she listens. Dad too. They listen. They never judge. They speak the truth in love. The second thing I have been given as a child of Gerry and Barbara is **Unconditional Love**.

Before I get into how I've received **Unconditional Love**, I have to brag on my Daddy. He showed unconditional love like you wouldn't believe. He's a romantic. I still live near my parents, on the same property, and I'll stop in the house and often, there will be fresh roses for Mom. Not because it's Valentine's Day, or her birthday. Just because he loves her. He's been doing it for 50 years. Loving Mom.

My favorite story about Dad's love for Mom happened the week I was born. When Paul and Christine, my older siblings, were born, Dad gave Mom a dozen roses. When I was born, money was tight, and I was born the day before payday. Dad couldn't afford a dozen roses. But, that didn't stop him from showing his love. As Mom held me in the hospital bed, he walked in with a single red rose. His example of unconditional love not only gave my mom tremendous value and security, it gave our family wholeness few ever have on this earth.

Oh, and he bought eleven more roses after payday.

Every Saturday, he would take one of us kids out. We would alternate weeks, and he would always get us something little. When we went on family vacations, the whole family went, including the clients from the group home. He and Mom never made apology or excuses, because they never saw the developmentally disabled as anything but God's sons and daughters.

Dad gave freely to all. He just gives and gives, and he's never stopped giving.

Boy, did he give to Gretchen. Not at the expense of anyone else, even though we joke in our house that Gretchen stole my "princess crown". I was the youngest. Key word, *Was*.

Then Gretchen came. I was Daddy's little girl. I could have easily become bitter and jealous over Dad's affection and attention toward Gretchen. I could have asked, "who is this interloper?" I'd be lying if I said there weren't moments that I felt unsettled by her displacement of me in the pecking order. But Dad and Mom's love was so strong and so unconditional I just learned to love Gretchen like they did. We became fast friends.

I couldn't help myself. She had a heart of gold. Though she couldn't see, could barely speak, and required constant care, there was a spark of life and sweetness to her that captivated me. From a physical standpoint, she had a very hard life. She was also emotionally very troubled. One of my most painful memories is how she would crawl across the carpeted parts of the floor to find the hardwood floor. Once there, she would bang her head on the floor.

I was in high school at the time. Gretchen was about 5 years old.

As the years passed, the challenges with Gretchen became part of daily life. When Gretchen made up her mind to not do something, she locked on. You couldn't break her will. She would pinch and hit, and Mom took plenty of abuse from Gretchen. Yet, Mom just kept loving her. We all did. Something really good and right happens in your soul when you love someone who really can't "do" anything for you.

Gretchen loved roughhousing and playing. She loved to wrestle, affectionately. She loved Peeps, you know those little marshmallow candy things that people get at Easter? She loved them, and so did I. When Peeps were in the house, she'd get so excited.

She loved music. She loved anything from worship music to Natalie Cole, and the standards. If Gretchen was struggling or getting agitated, we'd ask if she wanted her music. She would nod her head "yes", or smack her lips (which was her way of giving kisses) and we'd slip on her headphones. Her spirit would become calm as she swayed her head a little to the music.

I could make Gretchen laugh at the drop of a hat. We had a car called the "Gretchen Mobile" because it was the easiest car to load her in. It was a complete piece of crap car. It was clunky, even though it was new. No matter how new something is; if it's cheaply made, there is no point in buying it. I won't get started on how much junk people make nowadays. I used to jerk the steering wheel of the Gretchen Mobile and say, "I hate this car!" Gretchen would laugh hysterically.

Gretchen wore diapers until the day she died. As an adult, I would often be with her alone at the house. If I started to smell a stench, I would say, "Gretchen did you just take a dump in your pants?"

She would just grin at me like the Cheshire Cat. She knew what was going on and she would laugh. And I would take her into the other room to change her diaper. As I gagged over the smell, she just kept grinning like it was the greatest thing since sliced bread.

Some people might think that is disgusting. I call it **Unconditional Love**.

It's all I saw from Mom and Dad. To me, and to everyone, my parents are the most patient people who ever lived.

When anyone complained about people with special needs, Mom would say, "give them a break". Mom and Dad knew that no one chose to be developmentally disabled. And at the core, they are people with beautiful souls and desperate hearts. Hearts bursting with love and a deep desire to be loved, just like anyone else. That's what I learned from Mom and Dad.

I was raised in this environment. I got in trouble, sure, but I know I got off easier than my brother and sister. I'm the youngest. I'm still the baby, still Daddy's little girl. I am super blessed to have the parents I have and to live this life. I gave my parents a card this summer. They provide so much for me – a home, emotional support, friendship. It was kind of hard for me to give it to them. But I had to say thank you in a tangible way. Of course,

Mom started bawling her eyes out! She's so dramatic. Oh, how I love my Mom. How I love my Dad.

AT THE END OF GRETCHEN'S LIFE, she was on all the machines and stuff. The machines were keeping her body alive, but we all knew it was time for her to go to Heaven. Before we made the decision to turn off the machines, we decided to donate her organs to help others live. She would have liked that. The way it happens when you decide to "pull the plug" is someone from the family has to be there.

I volunteered to sit in with the doctors, along with my Mom and brother Paul. The three of us gathered in the operating room while the doctors disconnected everything that was keeping Gretchen alive. The three of us wept for the 20 minutes it took for her to stop breathing. As she slipped into eternity, we held each other and continued to cry.

After some time, the man in charge of the organ donation process came and took us into a side room. I imagine he does this every day. I can't imagine that he allows himself to get emotionally involved in situations. How could he function every day if he did?

When all the paperwork was completed and everything was official, he looked at us with tears in his eyes.

"I want you to know that it was an honor – it was my honor – and my privilege to work with your family. Your love is inspiring. Your love is the real thing. I've never met a family like yours before, and I've been doing this a long time."

That's all I've ever known. And that's all I've got to say.

Gretchen

Paul, Sarah, Sawyer and Hunter

Christine's Family

Tracy and Chicken Bone the goat

Philip and Gerry in Disney World

The whole family on Christmas Day at the farm

Philip and Christine

Christine's graduation party when she received her PhD

Grandchildren: Sydney, Caleb, Hunter and Sawyer

Barbara and Gerry sailing in Maine

The whole family - Disney vacation

Barbara and Gerry

4

Finding My Place

Sticks and stones may break my bones, but words will never hurt me.

WHAT A LOAD OF GARBAGE. The above expression might be one of the biggest lies ever told. Words hurt. They hit harder and they last longer than any stick or stone. Long after a broken bone is healed, words of anger, ridicule, bullying or doubt remain in our minds. In some cases, they remain in our head and heart an entire lifetime, dropping in unexpectedly, ruining a good day or wrecking a happy mood. In some lives, the damage is even worse. Sometimes, they cripple and crush the most precious thing of all – a human life. Words do much more than hurt people. Words kill our spirits and break our souls.

Finding the way to silence those words and replace them with the truth has taken me many years, and I'd love nothing more than to help you do the same. Breaking through the darkness that comes from damaging words is not easy but it is possible. And it's necessary. If we remain in bondage to the opinions of other people, we will be limited in our power to say yes to God. If we can't freely say yes to God, we will not be able find our place in Him. If we don't understand our place in Him, we will never be able to say yes to God. It's a paradox, but it's also the reality. As I've lived over seventy years and been a minister of the Gospel for over forty years, I've discovered that my identity in Christ is the release valve that takes away all the stress and pressure of other's expectations.

The truth is, before you or I can say yes to God, we have to understand who we are in Christ. I have discovered that the power of identity is paramount. It is the defining factor in having the power to say yes to God and the faith to "be confident of this very thing, that He who has begun a good work in you will complete it until the day of Jesus Christ." (Philippians 1:6)

As I write this chapter, I'm genuinely rethinking my theology. I know; that's a dangerous thing to admit in writing! But saying yes to God is dangerous. As I pray and think about how I found my place, and how to help others do the same, I am coming to the conclusion that most people struggle because they have a problem with their identity in Christ. Our inability to fully grasp the magnitude of His love and the power of His sacrifice on the cross makes it a constant challenge to not only say yes to Him but also to find our place in His work on earth. This is not a quick, cheap revelation. I have come to this place of understanding through many trials and tribulations, through many blessings and miracles. I am beginning to realize that I have come to this place so that I may help others find theirs. Before unveiling my rethought theology, here's a little personal history to explain how I got here.

EARLY IN MY LIFE, I struggled to overcome the negative opinions and attitudes of family members and neighbors. Like many people, I grew up in a place that looked for reasons to place blame and shame on my decisions and my behaviors. Worse than that, I grew up with influential voices reminding me that I didn't look as good as I should, or I talked too much. I faced a barrage of nitpicking and naysaying that penetrated my phony tough East Boston exterior and left deep holes in my heart and soul.

Sound familiar? I know there are many people who have lived through disrespectful, neglectful, and abusive families. I'm sure that most of you have your own tragedy to tell. I'm not here to rehash all the pain and abuse in my life, though a part of my story will no doubt help others. That's the point of telling the story – to inspire and inform, to shine a light and bring new life. I've included the critical experiences to show that saying yes to God will always bring (though sometimes it takes a long time) the best for your life and the lives of those you love and lead.

I was ridiculed for my weight. I was physically and sexually abused, when I was a young girl. I was wronged and I was mistreated. Mistreated is too weak a word for what happened to me. I was bruised and betrayed. I was helpless and I was humiliated. No one spoke for me. No one fought for me. Fear was my companion. Shame was my identity. All of these things were done to me, but none of them could compare to what Jesus wanted to do through me.

He understands being beaten. He understands betrayal. He understands rejection and ridicule. But Jesus did more than understand. Jesus became. He took all of those things, and so much more, on Himself at the cross. Jesus embodied every sin and shame so that our bodies and souls could be freed from the hurts of this life.

EVERYONE WANTS TO FIND his or her place in this world, and the world to come. Everyone wants to find the miraculous. Everyone wants strength, comfort and wisdom. You don't need this book to know this is true. But, you may need this book to understand a truth that took me quite a while to discover.

I've spent a lot of time as a pastoral counselor, particularly in the ministry of Inner Healing. As I mentioned, I've been rethinking my theology. In spite of all the years I've spent, or maybe because of it, I am coming to the conclusion that if we truly understood the power of the cross and truly believed God's Word, we wouldn't need inner healing. Some of my good friends and other pastors will probably disagree with me – some very strongly. I don't come to this conclusion lightly or easily. I come in awe of God and total respect for His Word and the Holy Spirit. But no matter what I do, I can't stop thinking about the words of Ephesians 2:10: "We are His workmanship, created in Christ Jesus for good works…"

We are created in Christ Jesus. Our freedom in Christ is all that is necessary for us to establish our true identity and discover our true purpose – the good works for which we were created. Too often, as I worked with individuals in the ministry of Inner Healing, we always ended up in the same place. No matter how much time we spent and talked and prayed, we kept looking back to find other hurts in need of healing. The truth is, we should forgive those hurts and move on. If all our time is spent investigating additional hurts, we become narcissists. We just keep thinking and talking about how we've been wounded and how we need more prayer to get over the past.

Take it from me, the past is the past. It's not coming back. I've experienced many times when the pursuit for deeper healing simply becomes a preoccupation with personal pride. And continually dredging it up for "healing" is just like ripping off a fresh scab. You are a new creation in Christ. As a new creation, you don't have any scabs. You don't have any wounds. You were made brand new by His extraordinary love and sacrifice.

Through the cross, we find freedom. Through the cross, we find our true identity. When we discover that He has liberated us, lock, stock, and barrel, we can run freely into His plan. We can run freely into the good work that He has created us for. We can say yes to Him without hesitation or reservation.

If you are carrying hurts or un-forgiveness, may I encourage you? Know who you are in Christ. Own who you are in Christ. Be who He believes you are – a beautiful, spectacular, radiant creation with one-of-a-kind gifts. Be who you are in Him – a powerful, faith-filled, determined giver of life to everyone you meet. As you fully discover your true identity in Christ, the journey of saying yes to God truly begins.

The closer you get to Him, the less the things of the world – especially people's opinions – matter. Your confidence and resolution will only grow. Your compassion and generosity will only increase. With each step, you will find your identity in Christ more clear and more real, because with each step your heart is becoming more and more like His. At the end of it all, saying yes to God becomes instantaneous, because there is nothing between your heart and His.

WE ARE ALL SEARCHING for our "place". As much as we tend to dismiss the need for position or place, on the inside we know the truth. The truth is there are few things that feel as good as the right fit, with the right people, and most importantly, the right affirmation from the people who matter.

What happens when we can't find that fit?

What happens when we don't hear those words of affirmation?

Once again, this is where saying yes to God proves to be both the answer and the mystery. It's the answer, because it's the simple truth. There isn't anyone in the Bible, or any great saint who has lived and died that didn't experience the freedom and the danger that comes when we say yes to God.

Abraham said "yes" when God asked him to sacrifice his only son.

Daniel said "yes" to God even when it meant certain death.

Esther said "yes" to God to save her nation or possibly lose her life.

Peter said "yes" to God when He was called to leave his career.

There are many more examples that I could include. Even if I tried to list them all, every reader of this book could name someone I overlooked. There is one person, however, we all would agree is the ultimate example. There is one person who said yes to God and whose "yes" enabled each of us to say the same.

That one person is the one and only Jesus. His prayer in the Garden of Gethsemane was the ultimate "yes" to God, for in those moments of deep reflection, anguish and, finally, surrender to God's will, Jesus undid what had been done in the Garden of Eden. He made it possible for man to be restored fully in relationship with God the Father.

Some may think that it was easy for Jesus to say yes to God. I don't think so. His "yes" was the ultimate not just because His sacrifice reconciled man to God; it was the ultimate because Jesus did it from His humanity. We lose sight of the truth that He did things while completely wrapped in His humanity. We can be dismissive of His work because it's convenient to think that it all came through His divine power. It was not His divine power that enabled Jesus to say yes to God – it was His perspective of the Divine – He was able to say yes because He watched His Father.

As Jesus explained to His disciples as recorded in John 5:19, "…Truly, truly, I say to you, the Son can do nothing of Himself, unless it is something He sees the Father doing; for whatever the Father does, these things the Son also does in like manner."

He only did what He saw the Father doing. Because Jesus had a perspective that only looked to God for direction, He was able to say yes to God. The more we strive to look to God for direction, the easier it will be – the easier it is – to say yes to Him.

The great men and women I mentioned above were no different from you or me. I think they were able to say yes to God no matter the consequences because of two things – (1) they renewed their mind, and (2) they kept the faith.

Finding our place isn't about a physical location. Finding our position isn't about a title at work. Finding our place and position is about our relationship to and with God. When we renew our mind and keep the faith, we find our place in His Kingdom, and we discover our position in His Creation.

Romans 12:1-2 explains, "I beseech you therefore, brethren, by the mercies of God, that you present your bodies a living sacrifice to

God, which is your reasonable service. And do not be conformed
to this world, **but be transformed by the renewing of your mind**,
that you may prove what is that good and acceptable and perfect
will of God."

THE APOSTLE PAUL WROTE these verses to a church in Rome —
and the passage remains instructive even today — to explain the importance
of renewing the mind in order to say yes to God.

It's no coincidence that the first part of the passage talks about saying
yes to God through the willing presentation of our bodies to be used in
God's service. Paul follows that instruction by telling us that it's our "reasonable service." As always, Paul didn't just write about what should be
done. He explained how it could be done. The challenge with saying yes
to God is that it runs counter to our personal desires and natural interests.
Paul knows this, which is why he inspires us to be transformed by renewing
our minds.

Renewing the mind doesn't mean changing your mind. It doesn't mean
losing your mind either! It means having the mind of Christ. Philippians 2:5-9 gives us an understanding of what it means to have the mind
of Christ. Because this point is so foundational to understanding what it
means — what it requires — to consistently and faithfully say yes to God, I
include the entire passage here:

> "Let this mind be in you which was also in Christ Jesus, who, being
> in the form of God, did not consider it robbery to be equal with
> God, but made Himself of no reputation, taking the form of a
> bondservant, and coming in the likeness of men. And being found
> in appearance as a man, He humbled Himself and became obedient
> to the point of death, even the death of the cross. Therefore God
> has also highly exalted Him and given Him the name that is above
> every name.

Jesus set the greatest example of what it means to say yes to God. He
said yes, and He was obedient, even to the death of the cross. Though He
was equal with God, Jesus lowered himself to the form of man and then
endured life on earth before ultimately being crucified for everyone's sins.
He couldn't accomplish His mission if He didn't have the right mind. He

had to be completely humble. This is the first step to renewing your mind, and this is the first step to saying yes to God.

Our mind is renewed when it's like the mind of Christ. Going back to Paul's words in Romans, we can present ourselves to be used by God when we are humble enough to follow Jesus's example and choose to follow God's direction over our fleshly desires. Renewing your mind starts by humbling yourself, trusting God, and obeying Him.

THE SECOND STEP to saying yes to God is keeping the faith. The renewal of your mind empowers you to say yes to God. Keeping your faith empowers you to say yes when everything around you, and just about everything in you, wants to say no.

Hebrews 11:1 reads, "Now faith is the substance of things hoped for, the evidence of things not seen." Think about this verse, which is often quoted, though I'm not sure it's fully understood. It makes a claim that an intangible attribute, faith, is the tangible substance of things that have yet to manifest in the physical world. It also claims that faith is the evidence of things still unseen. By virtue of the faith we carry and act on, we provide evidence for things yet to be made visible.

There will be many times in life when the things we are hoping for and the things we can't see seem light years away, while all the things we can see are horrible, difficult, even life-threatening situations. That's when faith keeps us going. Like the men and women above who said yes to God even when nothing made sense in their lives, we must choose to keep the faith that "He who began a good work in you will complete it."

That promise comes from Philippians 1:6, just a chapter before we are encouraged to renew our minds. It all works together. Renewing your mind, to be like Christ, and keeping the faith, like all the great saints who have come before, brings you to a position of strength in God that makes it possible for you to find your place in God. It gives you the power to trust Him in the storm. It helps you look up instead of around. Saying yes to God is the first step to transformation. It's the first step to renewing your mind and it's the first step to keeping the faith. Paradoxically, renewing your mind and keeping the faith is what helps you continue saying yes to God. And saying yes to God is how you truly, finally and fully, find your place.

5

Inner Healing

BEFORE I GET INTO this chapter I want to issue the following disclaimer: I have spent many years ministering with many wonderful people in the area of Inner Healing. I have many great and dear friends who are passionate about Inner Healing. I don't want some of my comments to be received as derogatory or negative. Indeed, I've experienced it first hand not only for myself, but for my daughter Gretchen, which I share in just a couple paragraphs below. I believe there is purpose and power in Inner Healing. However, if we allow it to become the only thing, or become the "be all, end all" for ministry, I don't believe that's proper.

As you read this chapter, please understand that I write these words after a long life of ministry and much prayer. My hope and desire is that we all say "yes" to God whatever He asks, whenever He asks it. I also hope that we have the grace and wisdom to understand that He moves in many ways and if we linger too long in a form or custom that He once moved in, we run the risk of becoming religious and stale. That is the thing I desire the least. Saying yes to God brings fresh life and allows the Holy Spirit to move. So, while I believe in Inner Healing, I also believe it is not meant to be a permanent place for people to live and operate. That is all. Now, on to the chapter.

THE AVERAGE WEIGHT OF A four-year-old girl is thirty-five pounds. When she was four, Gretchen weighed less than twenty pounds with failure to thrive. At that point, it was a miracle that she continued to live. A few months earlier, I attended a healing conference that specifically taught on Inner Healing. It was my introduction to this ministry. It was an emerging thought in the church and was often referred to as the "healing of memories." I was curious and motivated by the prospect of God working through the Spirit to bring healing to the pain and anguish many people carried every day as a result of tragic memories.

Though she couldn't communicate through typical speech, Gretchen's sounds and behavior made it very clear that she suffered from many painful memories. Deep in her subconscious, she carried wounds from rejection and trauma that few people ever experience. For months after she came to live with us, she never ever cried. Not one tear was shed. She expressed her frustration through self-abusive behavior. If she was hurting or upset, she would hit herself. Sometimes she would get down and bang her head against the hardwood floor. It was gut wrenching to see and hear her, unable to articulate her hurts.

After the first Inner Healing conference, I kept thinking about Gretchen. The next opportunity to attend an Inner Healing conference, I brought Gretchen with me. I was full of anticipation, expecting great healing to come for Gretchen.

The conference was great, and lots of people received great healings. The atmosphere of worship and faith was palpable. Gretchen received lots of prayer – people swarmed to pray for her healing. Though it was a wonderful conference, Gretchen apparently received no healing. I was a little disappointed as we left, but I resolved to continue believing she would receive Inner Healing.

After that conference, I went to visit my son, who was volunteering as a forest ranger in Oregon. The woodlands in the Pacific Northwest are beautiful, dramatic, and enchanting. Almost as soon as I got there, however, I came down with a severe case of ascites. Ascites is a dreadful condition associated with liver disease, and its primary symptom is the accumulation of fluid in the abdominal cavity. By the time I got home from my visit, there was so much fluid in my abdomen I looked like I was nine months pregnant.

I went straight to the hospital, and spent the next three weeks being treated for and recovering from ascites. By the time I was discharged from the hospital, it had been nearly a month since I was with Gretchen at the healing conference. I was exhausted, but grateful to be home, and hopeful that life would return to normal – whatever that meant!

Part of normal life was my bedtime routine with Gretchen. Every night, as I put her to bed, she would give me a little kiss and fall asleep. She was so peaceful and content as she drifted off to dreamland. The first night home from the hospital, I left her room with an extra bounce in my step. It was so good to be with my Gretchen. It was so good to be home.

The second night, as I put her to bed, we repeated our routine. As I kissed her goodnight and tucked her in, something completely unexpected and completely amazing happened. As I hovered over her, Gretchen reached her tiny hand up toward me. As she did, deep heart-wrenching sobs flooded from her mouth. Her body began to tremble as she cried. I immediately picked her up, carried her downstairs and laid her on my chest.

I prayed over her with all my heart, as she continued to sob and moan and tremble. I prayed for her to be healed from rejection from the womb. I prayed for her to be healed of the hurt caused by rejection from her parents. Any and every memory that I could think of that might have caused her trauma in the short time she'd been alive, I prayed for God to heal.

For the next three hours we were on the floor. I squeezed her close and told her over and over again how much God loved her. I told her how much I loved her, how she was special and treasured by everyone in our family. I told her she was wanted and cherished, that she was *needed*. She couldn't articulate her sadness, but through her tears that flowed freely that night, God intervened in her life and brought healing. He spoke directly to her spirit. After this encounter with God, she was truly healed. She started eating better, and she began to become healthy in body and soul.

That night is one of my most cherished memories of my entire life. That night was true Inner Healing for Gretchen. She knew who she was after that night. She knew God loved her, she knew He adored her, and many of those painful memories were erased from her mind.

I do believe in Inner Healing. I know what Gretchen experienced that night. It was a critical part of her growth and fulfillment of God's desires. But, it was a means to the end. Her healing. It was not an end in itself.

NO GRUDGES. Among the many remarkable strengths and gift of the developmentally delayed people we've cared for, I think the most beautiful is their purity of heart. They never hold a grudge. They don't dwell on the past. They simply and purely love, with a heart of relentless hopefulness.

I write this from a deep well of experience. Over thirty years have passed since our son Philip arrived as a poorly functioning toddler with

Down's Syndrome and lots of additional illnesses. In the past three decades, I have watched him live through continual sicknesses and physical limitations. I watched Philip embrace his father, the man who rejected him, after years without contact, without a hint of anger or resentment. I watched him become absolutely giddy at the prospect of meeting someone new and I watch him every week become thrilled at the opportunity to pray for anyone who will allow it.

There is much for us to learn from Philip's heart, and from the many people in our world just like him. Often ignored, patronized, or rejected, but almost always marginalized, the developmentally delayed are an extraordinary gift from God. They walk among us, yet they do not think like us. They share our environment, yet they prioritize the world unlike most of us. Some see this as a defect or an unfortunate tragedy. Nothing could be further from the truth. The truth is, they don't think like us and they don't share our priorities because, I believe, they think like children.

Children don't hesitate to help others in need. Children don't pause to consider what people will think if they pray in public. When they make decisions, they don't worry about the approval of others. Unlike us grown-ups, they haven't reached the point in life where the temporary earthly customs and opinions overwhelm the eternal heavenly priorities.

Philip has never reached that point, and I pray he never will. As a result, he has an ever-open connection to God. He has a direct line to heaven that allows him to pray for people and speak the most remarkable prophetic, healing words over their lives. Philip brings healing wherever he goes, although from our skewed perspective, he's the one that "needs healing" the most. Philip has never asked for inner healing or probably even thought about it. He approaches each day fresh and new, with the hope, love and faith of a child.

And that's his secret. That's the way we are supposed to approach God – like a child. But it's not really a secret, at least for those who read the Bible. Jesus told his disciples more than once that in order to enter the Kingdom of God, we must have the faith of a child. Children believe the most preposterous, dazzling, miraculous things – with ease. They believe in Santa Claus, they believe in fairies, and elves, and all the magical, mythical things that give life mystery and wonder.

As much as they believe in the world beyond what we can see and touch, children also believe in the world inside every human heart and mind. The world of the spirit and imagination is their preferred place of residence. Watch them play. Listen to them dream. Children speak with expectation and faith. Rare is the child who speaks about what "can't be" or the "worst case scenario." I don't think I've ever heard a child discuss planning for bad things. Children come to God with an open heart and an open mind. And, as a result, they are readily admitted into the Kingdom of God.

INNER HEALING is a loaded term in many circles of Christendom. In my experience it became and has become a sect unto itself. Conferences and seminars, books and sermons, all dedicated to the belief that Inner Healing is what we really need to fully become whole. I was a proponent of these meetings. I was an advocate for what I believed was the work of the Holy Spirit. I was deeply convinced that praying and working through Inner Healing was the only way a person could find freedom and forgiveness for major issues of abuse and neglect.

Over time, I've realized that I might have been wrong. Remember what I just wrote about the faith of a child? About an open mind? Well, this is one of those moments. As I've reflected and prayed, I believe God is revealing something different from what I've thought. I want to say yes to God. I am saying yes to God. With an open mind, I am willing to rethink everything I thought was important, and if God says I was wrong, I am willing to nod my head and say "yes." And I'm sharing it in real time, as I write this chapter. Stick with me; I think we can both learn something together.

I began to notice a pattern with the ministry of Inner Healing. Too often, I didn't see people moving on with life. Too often, we ended up in a pity party environment. I would pray with people and we would discuss (and I thought deal with) issues from the past. My desire was to bring them to a place of forgiveness. My desire was that the healing came as they actually blessed the people who had caused them pain. Unfortunately, most of what I've found over the years in the Inner Healing ministry and seminars is people just want to come and dump and vent their problems. They actually get to a place where they enjoy spilling their guts but they don't really want to clean up the mess.

I'm not trivializing the true pain and heartache that comes from major abuse or neglect. I'm not saying there aren't serious consequences that require professional care. But, I've seen the focus of Inner Healing too often be centered in the emotions of the person wronged, instead of the heart of God.

It's very easy and common to focus on the injured person. They are typically innocent victims and our natural tendency is to lavish them with compassion and support. But there comes a time to move on from spiritual and emotional triage. There comes a time to be discharged from the hospital of Inner Healing and to move back to a fully functioning, healthy, abundant life. As I listen to God, I believe He is saying it's sooner than we think. The reason it's sooner than we think is because of how He thinks. Let me explain.

TWO YEARS AGO, my husband Gerry had a very strange medical experience, and I observed it firsthand. I was leading a group seminar with Gerry. We were teaching in a School of Leadership at a church in Connecticut. The goal was to help people discover and achieve their purpose in life. We used the life of Nehemiah as the primary example and content.

It was always very fulfilling to assist people in maximizing their potential and improving their productivity. Gerry is a business genius, and helping others master their entrepreneurial endeavors is a great passion for him.

Well, we were gathered in a session and I noticed that Gerry kept repeating himself. He would talk for a minute, someone would ask a question, and then he would ask the room, "do you know your life purpose?" A few minutes would pass with different discussions and then Gerry would ask again, "do you know your life purpose?"

This happened many times during about a 30-40 minute period, until everyone noticed (especially me) that he wasn't repeating the question to make a point. He was repeating the question because he'd forgotten that he already asked it. As it kept happening, I began to grow concerned, then worried about him.

We got to the next break and I quickly took him aside. I was praying that he was ok, but I was nervous. With all my medical issues over the years, I didn't want to imagine Gerry incapacitated. Something was wrong, but I didn't know what it was. Clearly, Gerry's brain was not functioning properly.

"Gerry," I whispered as we huddled in a corner of the hotel conference area, "do you know where you live?"

He paused and looked at me for a little longer than he should have.

"Do you think it's Mystic?" he finally replied.

"Yes," I said. I was only slightly reassured.

"What are our children's names?" I asked.

As he stood there staring and thinking, I knew something was wrong. After a few minutes, he was able to remember three of our five children's names. Something was definitely off. Gerry is the best father I know. He loves his children more than his life. And yet, he couldn't think of all their names!

We rushed to the hospital, and I called our children. They all met me at the hospital. After lots of prayer and doctors' tests, he was diagnosed with transient global amnesia. Transient global amnesia is a sudden, temporary episode of memory loss that can't be attributed to a neurological condition. Fortunately, it is typically short in duration, and unlikely to be repeated.

It was a brief but intense scare. The next day, he was fine. But from that day to now, Gerry still has no recollection of that day. I have tried to prompt him by reminding him of the meetings. I told him about the hospital, about him forgetting his children's names. No matter how often we talk about that day, nothing rings a bell in his mind. For Gerry, it's as though that day never happened.

For all practical purposes, Gerry lost a day of his life. Though it happened (very traumatically, I might add) for the rest of us, Gerry still has no knowledge of that day.

I think it's kind of like that with God. When it comes to forgiveness and inner healing, God says we are a new creation. God has wiped away our past – as far as the east is from the west – which is why He can never remember our sins. Every time we bring them up, like me trying to remind Gerry about that day, God just has a blank stare. He probably says, "what are you talking about?"

You see; God has no recollection of our past because God only lives in the present. And He wants us to live in the present, in His presence.

WHAT'S MY POINT?

I'm glad you asked.

Here's the application. For those of us who are trying to get over the wrongs that have been done to us; for those of us trying to escape the pain of the past; we must learn how to be in His Presence. We must stop looking back at what we suffered and look to the One who bore all our sins. Take His word and meditate on it. Sit in His Presence and think about it. Ask, "How is this word going to change me?"

This is the beginning of healing. This is the beginning of saying yes to God. As I am realizing, His Presence, in the present, is everything. It's — dare I say? — the only thing. It's where we are and where He is. Our healing comes as a result of our desire to grow in relationship with Him. When we draw close to the love of our Heavenly Father, He begins to show us who we really are, and we find the identity that I wrote about in the previous chapter.

As we see who we really are, we pursue His love, and our healing comes. Our healing doesn't come from regurgitating the broken trust and the assaults we've suffered at the hands of others, but from meditating on the truth and affirmation we find in His word and the blessed unspeakable peace we feel in His presence.

This morning in my journal, I wrote these simple words: "Deep calls unto deep." As I pondered it, I realized the truth is that we think we are going after God, but really He's pursuing us. He's always been pursuing us. We love him because He first loved us. He initiates and I respond. Over and over, I say to my Abba father, my Heavenly Daddy, "yes."

With each yes, I am drawn deeper into His love. With each yes, I understand who I am in Him. This is healing. And I believe this is what God wants me to share.

Forgiveness is about approaching each day fresh and new, like our son Philip does. Forgiveness is about forgetting those hurts. Not by pretending they never happened, like Gerry's amnesia, but by focusing so much on the heart of God we begin to be overwhelmed by His grace for everyone.

When we focus on the heart of God, we are drawn closer to Him. He desires relationship with us, His children. In and through His love, we find true healing. We overcome the ritual and the religion that too often tries to substitute itself for the true heart of God in our lives. In many ways, Inner Healing has become a substitute for what God desires.

I am not saying that all Inner Healing is wrong, but often I have seen it presented in much the same way as many good things, with meaningful truth and powerful revelation. Yet when it becomes an end to itself, instead of a means to an end, it falls short, like many good things, of the greatness of God. When we approach our loving Heavenly Father in the present, in

His presence, we discover that the past no longer has a hold on us. When we follow after God's heart alone, we find the future is free and clear.

AS I EXPLORE more fully this notion of forgiveness and Inner Healing, I have come to a conclusion. I have realized that forgiveness is the key that unlocks healing. It is the only thing that works. Therapy is fine, counseling is encouraging, but until we truly forgive we will never experience Inner Healing.

"Easy for you to say," I can hear some of you saying. "You don't understand what I've been through. You don't understand what so-and-so did to me."

You're right. I don't understand. But playing "can you top this" about our hurts is exactly the problem I was getting at in my explanation of why I believe the Inner Healing movement doesn't always work. When we constantly rehearse and rehash our pains, we won't move past them. We won't experience God's healing and we are unable to become agents of His love in our communities.

Be patient as you consider this section of the book. I am more convinced than ever of its truth and its power. Why? Because I have experienced it in my own life and I believe it is a life-changing revelation.

I was hurt by the Catholic Church, or more rightly, by people who worked in and for the Church. I saw others mistreated by the Catholic Church, and I had my own unhealthy interactions with several priests. The truth is, I have had many moments that led to a build up of resentment and hostility toward the Church.

I know many people who are, like I was, angry and bitter toward the Catholic Church. I'm not alone, and I could commiserate with like-offended people and never move on. That would be a grave mistake and a great disappointment to God, my Father.

The mistake I made is a common one. Over time, I equated the few people who hurt me with the entire Catholic Church. That would be like having a bad meal at a local Pizza Hut and from that experience declaring that all Pizza Huts and all their employees were no good. It's easy to laugh at that exaggeration, but it's a true comparison.

For example, I listen to a character on the radio who calls himself The Catholic Guy. He's a satirical guy who I'm sure is intentionally bombastic, but the reality is his comments are a reflection of stereotypes that only serve to divide the people of God. On occasion, I find him to be very crude and very demeaning toward Protestants. It's unbelievable. As I listen to him, I begin to get upset, and wonder if he is going to correct what he is saying. Unfortunately, he doesn't.

Though I can't listen to him for too long, I did begin to understand that I was no different in my animosity toward the Catholic Church. As much as his comments about Protestants were ignorant and disrespectful, my anger toward the Catholic Church was no better. I was doing the same thing – labeling everyone by a single identity. Because of a handful of offenses from a handful of people, I chose to reject an entire organization of wonderful people who were serving God and loving others.

As I realized my anger was spilling over into my life and really was preventing my growth in God, I finally broke down and forgave. But, forgiveness is not just saying, "I forgive." It's also asking God to forgive us for our own bitter root of judgment. If we've allowed condemnation of others to slip into our hearts, we have to ask God for forgiveness. Then you can begin forgiving others, which is more than just saying a few words. It's a process that includes multiple steps: forgiving, releasing, and blessing. Forgive the injury. Release the offense. Bless the offender.

Let me repeat that: Forgive the injury. Release the offense. Bless the offender. This is the process that I've discovered as the only way to find real Inner Healing and to bring peace – finally – into my life. I put it into practice. Every time I walked by a Catholic church, I repeated forgiveness and blessing. I released the offense.

Even more importantly, the real issue in the midst of my forgiveness was that I had to ask God's forgiveness. I allowed a bitter root of judgment to grow in my spirit and in my life. Like a mushroom blooming overnight, that bitter root would spring up inside me. It needed to be completely removed from my life. It came up often and that is when I realized I still needed to forgive, and to ask for God's forgiveness.

When we proclaim blessing over something that is negative in our life, it begins to change. Not overnight, but gradually, over time, God changes our heart. He brings full and complete healing. Whatever we speak out will become true. We are to pray for our enemies because God knows that's the only way change will come. Be a person that forgives and speaks blessing into painful situations. The truth is Jesus loves us all. It may be hard to comprehend, but He loves the person who hurt you as much as He loves you. The truth is, He loves the Islamic terrorist as much as He loves the most holy Christian.

As I reflect on Jesus' response to Peter about forgiveness, I realized that I've often misunderstood what He meant. Here's the familiar passage, found in Matthew 18:21-22:

> "Then Peter came to Jesus and asked, 'Lord, how many times should I forgive my brother or sister who sins against me? Up to seven times?' Jesus answered, 'I tell you, not seven times, but seventy times seven!'"

In this exchange, Jesus responds to what Peter believes to be an exceptional answer, 7 times, with an extreme answer – seventy times seven – 490 times! Jesus didn't mean that we should count to four hundred and ninety and then stop forgiving. He was helping the disciples understand that forgiveness never stops. The disciples grew up in a legalistic culture and were used to following rules and "checking the box" to bring religious affirmation. Jesus broke all that. He wasn't looking for religious affirmation or form of tradition. He was looking for spiritual restoration and reconciliation.

Over the years, I've thought that the phrase "seventy times seven" was referring to the number of offenses we should forgive. As I've experienced true healing through the process of forgiving the Catholic church, **I now believe seventy times seven is a description of the truth that *I have to repeatedly forgive the same offense.***

Each time the pain and hurt, or resentment and bitterness resurfaced in my mind and heart, I consciously and verbally forgave. I am sure it's now passed 490 times that I've forgiven the same offense. Each time, it gets easier to release the hurt and bless the offender. Each time I forgave, released, and blessed, I could feel the presence of God. I could hear the Holy Spirit encouraging me. I could feel the Father's love, flooding my soul and aligning my spirit closer to His heart.

I must take captive every thought. I can't respond in my flesh. For example, there was a man with whom I once worked who ended up being extremely dishonest and caused a great deal of pain to many people. When I think of him, even though it's been many years, I have to choose to forgive. I have to be mature and follow the Scripture. If I have to run to a counseling session every time I'm reminded of some injury or slight that caused offense, I am not growing the strength I need to live fully for God.

THE DECISION I MADE to forgive the Catholic Church, and my continual willingness to keep forgiving and blessing brought about a transformative experience in my life. There was a time in my life when the sight of anything or anyone affiliated with Catholicism would instantly send a surge of anger into my spirit. It's remarkable that today I find myself defending the Catholic Church to people who believe that everyone in the Catholic Church is wrong!

I realized that my need to forgive was much more important than my need to be "right." I realized that speaking blessing honored God and brought deep healing – deeper than anything I experienced when I sat around talking about my wounds. As I continually forgave and blessed, I couldn't help but see the good in everything, even people in the church who had deeply offended me.

But that's what happens when you choose not to throw the baby out with the bath water. Boy, that sure does happen a lot. We let our emotions run roughshod over the truth of God's Word. We focus on ourselves and ignore the Holy Spirit. In the process, we diminish the power of God in our lives. We believe the lie that persuades us to abandon God's perspective.

That's the root of it all. Deception. Untruth. Lies. Behind every negative emotion is a lie. What's sad is it doesn't even take a complete fabrication. Most often, it's a simple exaggeration that sweeps us away and carries us off into a place of self-absorbed pity and constant complaint.

The longer we listen to the lie, the longer we remain unhealed. The sooner we replace the lie with the truth, the quicker we become healed. We must speak the truth to overcome the lie. We may not have the right words, but God's Word is always right. It's the ultimate truth, and it's the ultimate weapon against the lies that prevent Inner Healing from taking place.

A great example is the lie of unworthiness. At some point in life, everyone experiences doubts that cause him or her to feel inferior or incapable of doing something great. Is there any limiting factor in humanity more widespread than negative self-image? And yet, we all believe the lie that tells us we don't measure up. Replace that lie with God's truth. In Psalm

139:13-18, we read the greatest description of every human who ever lived. In this passage, we read the truth. The unmistakable, undeniable truth of how precious every person is in the eyes of God:

For you (God) created my inmost being;
You knit me together in my mother's womb.
I praise you because I am fearfully and wonderfully made;
Your works are wonderful, I know that full well.
My frame was not hidden from you
When I was made in the secret place,
When I was woven together in the depths of the earth.
Your eyes saw my unformed body;
All the days ordained for me were written in your book
Before one of them came to be.
How precious to me are your thoughts, God!
How vast is the sum of them!
Were I to count them,
They would outnumber the grains of sand –
When I awake, I am still with you.

God's thoughts toward you outnumber the grains of sand! What an amazing thought and an incredible truth that should shatter every lie that you're not good enough. Replace the lie of unworthiness with the truth that you are wonderfully made. This is just one example of the importance of replacing lies with His truth. And this should be how you find full and complete healing. While Inner Healing certainly helps and it may bring a person to a discovery of God's love, it shouldn't become the "be all, end all" for how we restore purpose to our lives and become healed of our wounds and pain.

Look to God for the answer. Take His word and meditate on it. Sit in His presence and ask yourself, "How is this Word changing me?" Remember, His Word is sharper than any two-edged sword. It can divide and drive to the heart of the matter like nothing else ever will. As you meditate on His word, the healing comes. He begins to show us who we really are in Him, and that brings the transformative healing that everyone's heart longs to experience.

I encourage you to think about the hurts that are close to the surface today. Not to replay the offense or have a pity party. But to forgive, release and bless. Begin to follow these steps every time offense rears its ugly head. Every time you begin to hear that little voice in your mind whisper, "It's unfair. It's not right. You were mistreated, cheated and abused." I encourage you to cut it off with your own voice, declaring, "I forgive. I love as God loved me. I release the pain. I bless the person and I pray for their blessing from God."

At first, it may be difficult. But I promise if you'll stay in the present, in His presence, and choose to forgive, release and bless, you'll discover the true healing that lasts. You'll experience the kind of permanent healing and reconciliation that brings freedom that God intends and only God can give.

6

A Pioneer's Life

ONCE UPON A TIME, almost everything you own and almost every path you take did not exist. Whether it's the car you drive or the roads you drive upon, there was a day in the not-so-distant past, before modern innovations, when neither the car nor the roads were available for human transportation. Not so long ago, roads were dirt or gravel, and the movement of people and freight were accomplished by animals pulling rough-hewn carts.

At some point in time, someone thought, "There's got to be a better way." And because they believed this to be true, they began to innovate. They began to think and experiment and risk and wonder and imagine improvements yet to be. They began to dream and explore and tinker and gamble and throw caution to the wind.

They began to pioneer.

I have a great passion for pioneering and for those who, like me, are often on the front lines of the work of God. I don't write that with any arrogance, mind you, I simply understand the way God designed me. I was created to pioneer.

We live in an area of America that was settled by pioneers (I suppose just about everyone in America does). Brave men and women endured severe hardships and extremely limiting environments to build a new life out of a hard, bitter cold, land. I live in Connecticut, the Constitution State, founded by a group led by Thomas Hooker. Most of the early settlers were Dutch and their no-nonsense demeanor and self-deprecating approach to life still informs our culture today.

Back in the 1630's, there weren't any freeways. Refrigeration or pasteurization didn't exist. There were no planes, trains, or automobiles. There was no telegraph, telephone, or satellite television. There were no computers. There was no internet. I could go on and on with the list of modern conveniences that were not available to the pioneers of the 1600's. I belabor the point, however, to set up the analogy.

Pioneering for God requires the same character traits as those who pioneered to establish our nation. Focus, fortitude, and faith are just a few of the qualities necessary to forge in a spiritual or natural wilderness. One thing I've noticed - pioneers are often injured and sometimes they get shot. They face tremendous obstacles, including forces opposed to their advancement.

Pioneers walk through difficulties. Much like carving a path through the forest, the pioneer is in front, slowly but consistently hacking away at the brush, all the while knowing that one day, many others will follow behind on a clear and much easier to follow road. As Jesus, the author and finisher of our faith, went to the cross because of the joy (us) set before Him, pioneers take the heat because of the vision of the people who will one day benefit from the actions of the pioneer.

SUCH WAS THE CASE when we first started our group home. This was long before today's environment of support and encouragement for the disabled. In fact, we were the second community training home in the entire state of Connecticut. We began in our own home, with four clients. All of them were transfers from institutions. They were coming from a medicated, isolated situation. Interaction with people was very limited. Love was foreign. Compassion was rare. We had little money and very little experience. We said yes to God in a big way. So much was unknown. Not just for us, but for the community in general.

We didn't have room in our house to take in any more young people, but our hearts still had lots of room to love. We had to get a bigger house. So, I started looking. And I found a house. Now, paying for it was a different matter altogether but money never stopped us from believing that God would come through. As is usually the case, I opened my big mouth and God took me up on it.

The house that I found was for sale. It's the house I mentioned earlier, the large Victorian mansion. It was beautiful. It was a perfect representation of classic old architecture, with wide wooden siding and clapboard shutters. Even though it was rough, it retained its elegance. A well-known politician, Senator Chris Dodd, owned the house. It needed some work, but oh, the potential!

I walked in the front door and said, "I'm going to buy this house." The list price on the house was $65,000. This was over 30 years ago, so we're talking real money. Gerry told me we could manage a mortgage up to $45,000. Forty-five thousand, sixty-five thousand, it was all numbers to me. We had nothing, so what difference was $20,000?

Saying yes to God often defies rational thought. If His miracles could fit inside a rational mind, they wouldn't be miracles, you know? I was confident about this house because I knew we were following God's direction in helping disabled people find a place where they would be loved and respected. We were living the gospel as we gave them the dignity they deserved.

We made the offer on the house for $65,000. We needed $10,000 for a down payment. We had zero.

That's right, we had no money.

We were in the right place for God to work. The first miracle was maybe the most incredible. For years, my mother, who never gave me anything but grief, mostly told me how I couldn't do anything. Her repeated discouragement of my ambitions was one of the hardest things I ever forgave. We had finally reconciled a few years before, I think in part because my relationship with God fulfilled her dream of having a member of the clergy in the family. Mom always wanted a son to become a priest or a daughter to become a nun.

As I told her about the home and the need to care for so many disadvantaged disabled people, God worked in her heart. Initially, she was apprehensive. We were entering the unknown by saying yes to God and caring for the severely disabled. But, that's the life of a pioneer. And pioneers inspire others. In this case, even my own mother! When I expected her to laugh or scold or tell me to abandon the idea of buying the home, she did the complete opposite.

She told me that she thought it was a good thing. She told me that we were making a difference in people's lives and that was important. Then she told me she was going to give us $2,500 toward the down payment! I could have been knocked over with the slightest breeze. I was in shock! Saying yes to God had led to my mother, for the first time in my life, saying yes to me.

Once Mom was on board and contributed, I felt like we couldn't be stopped. I just knew it was all going to work out. And then, nothing else opened up for additional funds. Time was running out. I asked for help, and finally we were able to get another $2,500 from a good friend. As the day of the closing approached we still needed $5,000 for our down payment. I prayed all the more but it didn't look good. Of course, my flesh wanted me to give in. But, every time I was tempted to throw in the towel, I looked at our wonderful residents, who had been stuck in a little room with little exercise and minimal care, who now were with us in a loving family, worshiping God and living full lives. I couldn't give up. And neither would God.

The day before the closing, I received a phone call. It was from the accountant of the Catholic diocese where we lived and where we ministered. I couldn't imagine what he would want. He was an older man, very stoic in demeanor, and I do admit, quite intimidating. Besides his appearance, he was well known for being very stingy. If you want to imagine him, basically, just picture Ebenezer Scrooge in a Catholic church, and that was my impression of this man. Of course, he was the perfect person to manage money because he wouldn't spend a dime more than absolutely necessary.

"I have never been so happy to give someone money as I am to give it to you," he said as I sat down in his office.

"What?" I replied, genuinely surprised by his smile. I don't think I'd seen him smile – ever.

"That's right," he replied. "I am thrilled to give you this check."

Somehow he had found out about us buying the house. To this day, I don't know how God got the message to this man. But He did, just in the nick of time.

He reached over his desk and handed me a check. As my shaking hands took it from him, my eyes leaped to the right side of the check. There in black ink, in clear bold handwriting, was the following amount: $5,000.00

We had our $10,000 down payment. With less than 24 hours to go, we had the money we needed. And, just as I'd said the moment I first walked into the old Victorian mansion, we bought that house. Sometimes being a pioneer means walking a tightrope of faith, it means coming down to the wire, yet never backing down. Being a pioneer means taking the risks that few other people would take. Being a pioneer means saying yes to God. And then, watching Him say yes to you.

ONE TRUTH of the pioneer life is limited affirmation. In fact, in many instances, the opposite sentiment is expressed. A pioneer faces criticism, ridicule and rejection on a regular basis. Sometimes that criticism can come from a very respected source, making the pioneer feel foolish, or even consider quitting. Once such example is the Wright Brothers, the inventors of the airplane, and the predecessors of modern flight. Modern flight has ushered in a dramatic change in the human experience and has literally made it possible to visit places that once were impossible to reach without extraordinary effort and expense.

Yet, if the Wright Brothers had listened to Thomas Edison, a pioneer in his own right and one of the most brilliant men to ever live, they might have abandoned their search for air travel before it ever got off the ground (sorry, I couldn't resist the pun).

When asked by the *New York World* newspaper about the possibility of human flight, Thomas Edison said, "It is apparent to me that the possibilities of the aeroplane, which two or three years ago were thought to hold the solution to the flying machine problem, have been exhausted, and that we must turn elsewhere."[9]

Fortunately for all of us, the Wright Brothers ignored Mr. Edison's criticism. Though they faced lots of challenges, they persisted, and less than a decade after Edison's quote, the Wright Brothers achieved their goal. Less than a century later, in the United States alone, there are 87,000+ flights a day!

The pioneer life is no different and the possibilities of doing great things for God are no less significant. As a woman in ministry, the determination of a pioneer's spirit has been an absolute necessity. For me, saying yes to God has often meant ignoring lots of voices telling me "no."

Early on, I experienced delay and even outright denial for access to certain levels of ministry simply because I was a woman. I realize that even now there are many churches that refuse to ordain women, but thirty years ago, it was exceedingly rare. I was aware of the barriers, but I wasn't always focused on them. I was blessed to work with some forward-thinking pastors and I was optimistic. I expected others to join the open-minded approach and accept women more readily into the ministry. I was wrong!

Even the men with whom I ministered often secretly held the conviction that women were not meant to hold certain positions of leadership or authority within the church. One conversation in particular really surprised me. I was part of a team ministering to teenagers at a youth conference in South America about 17 years ago. It was an amazing time of ministry. Over 1,000 teenagers worshiped God with such fervency that the dirt floor turned into a cloud of dust waist high. The authentic move of the Holy Spirit was beautiful and miraculous.

During a break in the conference, Phil Strout, who is now the leader of the Vineyard Movement in America pulled me aside. I didn't know what he wanted to talk about. Maybe how exciting it was to see so many young people on fire for Jesus? Maybe he wanted to talk about future ministry opportunities? No. Nothing of the sort.

After a minute of small talk, he looked me in the eye and he said, "I want to ask your forgiveness."

I wasn't sure what he meant, and I'm sure the look on my face showed it. He continued to speak, and as he did, I understood why he wanted my forgiveness.

"For a long time," he continued, "I was not pleased that you were a woman pastor. I didn't like the idea of women as pastors. But now, after ministering together, I realize that you are a better pastor than I could have ever been. I want to ask your forgiveness for the way I thought about you."

I was surprised but I accepted his apology. I told him that I forgave him. Pioneering always includes resistance. But that's what God asked me to be. Pioneering is what He asked me to do. As soon as I said yes to God, I entered a place that couldn't be supported by the applause of men. I had to be supported by the voice of God. When you pioneer, you are saying yes to God. When you say "yes" to God, be prepared to have a dozen voices (or more) discrediting or discouraging you. But, also be prepared to have God show up in the nick of time.

Be positioned to hear God's voice above all the rest. It's the only way to find your direction and the only way to set your course. The life of a pioneer may be harder than others, but it also allows you to be the first to see new territory. Saying yes to God might just be the most exhilarating adventure you've ever experienced and I'm certain life lived any other way will never compare.

7

Just In Time

"JESUS has a very special love for you. As for me, the silence and the emptiness is so great that I look and do not see, listen and do not hear."

THE SENTENCE ABOVE is a direct quote from the most unlikely of sources. It's not from a bitter malcontent. A mistreated churchgoer didn't utter those words. They didn't come from the lips of someone who'd been betrayed, disappointed or was otherwise cynical about the existence of God or Jesus. No, the above quote came from none other than the most widely respected nun of the past 100 years. Mother Teresa wrote those words, in a letter she wrote to Reverend Michael Van DerPeet in September 1979.[10]

She was expressing what came to be a very familiar experience. The Blessed Teresa of Calcutta spent most of her 87 years of life giving tirelessly to the least desirable people on earth. One would think that a woman who exhausted her life in charity would feel God in her life every day, if not every moment. Yet, somehow, the opposite is true. Maybe it's a paradox, I'm not sure. But, I know in my own life I have had moments where I wasn't sure where God was. It's hard to say yes to God if you feel like He's not even speaking.

C.S. Lewis illustrates the difficulty of believing in God when He doesn't seem very close in his essay, *The Efficacy of Prayer*. The reality is we don't just get whatever we ask for from God. And, sometimes, He flat out denies a request that we desperately want. But, as C.S. Lewis points out, the same thing once happened to Jesus.

"Prayer is not a machine. It is not magic. The refused prayer of Christ in Gethsemane is (proof) enough to that. Does God then forsake those who serve Him best? Well, He who served God best of all said, near His tortured death, 'Why hast thou forsaken me?'" [11]

IS IT POSSIBLE that seasons of the Christian life are spent without the direct, tangible presence of God? If Mother Teresa and C.S. Lewis experienced the agony of isolation from God's presence, does God's nature and manner of teaching us how to live include periods of loneliness? If so, what is His purpose in it all?

I don't know everything about God, but I do know that I can take Him at His word. I can believe what He says, and that makes it much easier to say "yes" to Him. One thing I know for certain is that He will never leave us or forsake us. In Isaiah 49:15-16, God says, "I will never forget you. Behold, I have written your name on the palms of my hands."

Like Mother Teresa, I believe we all have moments of loneliness and doubt, but we also think we're the only ones experiencing such feelings. Many times, I've had people hear about our family, or see us in years gone by with Gretchen, and they say, "Oh, I could never do what you do!"

The impression I get is that people think we are holier than others or we have some supernatural abilities. The truth is God gives us grace to do it. Everyone is called to do something different, and for each person God will show up when necessary – usually far after we believe He should.

The reality is there were many times I thought, "Life would have been so much easier if we hadn't adopted Gretchen." Other days, I cried out, "What the heck have we gotten ourselves into?"

Yet, God knew. More accurately, God knows.

GEORGE MULLER, a well-known man of God from the 1800's, is perhaps the embodiment of living in faith. He trusted God to show up in the nick of time. Over the course of his life, he established orphanages and schools, and by the time he died, had established 117 schools, providing Christian education to over 120,000 children.

It was said that he prayed about everything and he believed that every prayer would be answered. Books are filled with stories about the orphanages needing food, or equipment needing repair, and Muller's response was always to pray. And God would provide. An oft-shared story from his life was a time when there was no food in the orphanage. When morning came, George set all the children down at the kitchen tables. They prayed and gave God thanks for the meal – which they didn't have!

Minutes later, there was a knock at the door. A baker arrived with enough fresh bread to feed everyone. Moments after the baker left, a milkman arrived with lots of fresh milk that was going to be wasted if they didn't take it, because the milkman's truck had broken down.

God answers prayers. And He often answers them in the nick of time. George Muller's life showed this to be true time and time again. We've learned it for ourselves, as well.

GOD USUALLY showed up in the nick of time for us in the area of financial provision. One day, when we still lived in the community Ave Maria House, we were working for the Office of Ministry to the Developmentally Disabled, and a friend came to visit. She was a good friend, and a believer in Jesus Christ. But, like many Christians, she had yet to cross over to fully saying yes to God. She still kept her eyes on the material world instead of looking to Heaven for her needs.

"How on earth do you pay your bills?" she asked. She knew what we had sacrificed and she knew the expense of caring for a number of special needs children, in addition to our own.

Before I could answer, there was a knock at the door.

"Excuse me for a moment," I said, and went to the front door.

I opened the door to see a man I'd never met. I didn't know why he'd shown up.

Maybe he's here to see Gerry, I thought.

"You don't know me," he said. "I heard about your community home and I'd like to leave you a donation."

"Oh, please come in," I replied. "Would you like some coffee?"

We walked into the kitchen but he declined my coffee.

"No thank you," he replied. "How much do you want for a donation?" he asked.

I told him to give whatever he felt he should.

I glanced at the table, where I saw the most recent bill for our heating oil. I didn't say anything else, as the man had already pulled out his checkbook.

He wrote the check, handed it to me and left without saying another word.

"Thank you," I said, as he walked away.

I turned back into the house, not having looked at the check yet. My friend was sitting in the corner, where I'd left her, eyes wide.

"What did he give you?" she asked.

I unfolded the check, and it was the exact amount of our heating oil bill.

"As I was about to say," I whispered to my friend, "This," I held up the check, "is how we pay our bills."

SOMETIMES, GOD SHOWS UP just in time for someone else, but He uses me to accomplish the rescue mission. I think if we are patient and prayerful, we discover so often our own inconveniences or discomfort opens a door to assist another. If you study the life of Jesus, you'll find that often He was on His way to somewhere when He was interrupted by a person in need. In my own life, I've discovered that God's nick of time for people is typically an interrupted time for me.

As I've said before, I don't believe God wants me to be sick. I believe God's ultimate desire is for everyone to be healed and whole. But, I believe God works all things for His purpose, and my illnesses are no exception. In the midst of my suffering, I've been used by God to show up – sometimes literally – just in time.

ONE STORY of this phenomenon sticks in my mind even now. I had been admitted to the hospital once again. As I often did, I used the time to study the Bible, listen to preachers and teachers on cassette tape (I graduated to CD's recently), and softly worship. It doesn't take long for patients to hear and learn that I'm a minister.

After a few days during this particular stay, a very elderly woman came to me in the hallway while I was getting a little exercise by walking the halls. She explained that her husband was nearing the end. They had been married many, many years and her eyes were full of compassion. Her own body was tired and hunched, but her health was still good. It was obvious she had spent many nights caring and praying for her husband. She asked me if I could come in and pray with him.

As we entered the room, I could sense that his time was almost up. There is a tangible presence in the atmosphere when death is near. My mood was reverent but my heart was exuberant to minister to this dear dying man. Monitors were beeping and IV cords entangled his frail arms. He couldn't speak, so I asked him to blink one time for "no" and two times for "yes."

"Do you understand me?" I asked softly as I slid into a chair alongside his bed.

His tired puffy eyes blinked twice. The skin on his face was like paper, so thin. Fine blue veins crisscrossed his cheeks and forehead like little rivers.

"Would you like to pray to ask Jesus to be your Saviour?" I asked.

He slowly but deliberately blinked twice. He opened his eyes as wide as he could between blinks to be sure I knew he was saying yes.

I smiled and looked up at his dear wife. She was near his head, leaning over the bed, one hand tenderly stroking his hair, the other resting on his bony shoulder.

To be in a moment like that is a high honor and a humbling experience. There I was, leading this man in prayer to accept Jesus, as he was on the verge of meeting Jesus face-to-face.

I asked him to agree with me in prayer. I prayed the sinner's prayer and then looked at him.

"Do you agree with what I just prayed?" I asked.

He blinked twice again. Then a soft sigh escaped his lips and his body relaxed. The peace of God reigned in his body and in that room.

A few minutes later, a nurse entered, and I excused myself.

A few hours later, word came to me that he'd passed away.

It seems that no matter what we go through we can always find a way to bring the love of God into a person's life. I was just walking the hallway, and was interrupted. But, it was the best kind of interruption – a God interruption. Of course, I'd rather not be in the hospital. But, if I'm going to be there, I'm going to bring people to Jesus. Sometimes, I get to bring Him just in the nick of time.

ONE FINAL EXAMPLE (though I have dozens I could share) happened rather recently. For months Gerry and I, along with four other couples who were life-long friends, had planned for a trip to Italy. It was going to be a refreshing time, a once-in-a-lifetime trip. I was so excited to go. As the day drew near, I started to feel sick. The departure day was on a Friday.

It was Monday morning. As I woke up, I didn't feel good at all.

"Please God," I prayed, "don't let me miss the trip to Italy!"

"What did you just say?" Gerry asked.

"I just want to go to Italy, Gerry." I said as I sat up in the bed.

He looked at me. Rather, he studied me. I couldn't fake it. I couldn't hide it. He knows me inside and out.

"Come on, let's go to the hospital," Gerry said. "It's probably nothing. Let's just go have the doctors check you out and make sure you're all well to go to Italy," he tried to reassure me.

We got the hospital and they did some preliminary tests. The doctors at the hospital decided I should go to Yale. They put me in the back of an ambulance, for an hour-long bumpy ride. That was no fun!

When I arrived at Yale, all my vitals were fine. I honestly felt fine. As we waited, suddenly I started getting chills and started shaking violently. My whole body was convulsing and I thought I was having a seizure. It was uncontrollable. The doctors and nurses rushed to me. Suddenly, my temperature spiked to 105. They pushed me down the hall to a private room, where I was rapidly packed in ice.

The fever started dropping, but I was still shaking.

A few hours later, they had the diagnosis: I had a blood infection.

"I'm still going to Italy," I told anyone who would listen.

Tuesday, things weren't improving. It was miserable. I still had hope I was going to Italy, but no one else believed.

But, God still worked, as He always does. The hospital at Yale is a teaching hospital, naturally, and I got to teach the rising doctors about God. A small group of them would enter, review my records and ask me questions. One of the most common questions, after the boring stuff about symptoms and treatments, was, "How did you survive this much illness for so many years?"

I think they were genuinely stunned that a woman could live for the better part of three decades with major illness, serious surgery, and constant complications from all of the above.

"Only because of God," I would reply, which always made me smile, even when I hurt like hell.

Some of the doctors would nod their head. One nurse gave her life to Jesus.

On Wednesday, the doctors told me that I wasn't going to make the trip to Italy. The first thought that God dropped in my head was from the apostle Paul. In Philippians 4:11, he writes, "be content in all things." (my paraphrase)

When you've been in the hospital as often as I have, contentment in Christ is a necessity. It's a true survival mechanism that becomes a thriving mechanism.

On Wednesday, they moved me to a Rehab Center. It was a dump. It was musty smelling, the ceiling tiles had water stains that looked like amoeba crawling around the wretched florescent lights. I was loaded up with antibiotics, the food was horrible, and the room I was in had two competing TVs on the wall. In the morning it was The Price is Right v. Judge Judy. At night, it was The Wheel of Fortune v. Entertainment Tonight. I was not in a good mood.

But there's no sense griping and complaining about everything. God can and does use whatever we go through in life. Saying yes to God means surrendering to Him. Saying yes to God is the way that we discover a blessing in the shadows of life.

So, there I was, on Wednesday, two days before I was supposed to go on the trip of my life to Italy. I wasn't going. I knew it in my heart. I kinda knew it on Monday.

"Ok, God, what's the purpose here?" I asked. I felt like God was going to bring someone to me. I earnestly prayed for the next two days for the woman who was my roommate to have a genuine salvation experience.

She was a kind lady with a gentle timid spirit.

We made small talk, and then laid there for an hour or so.

"What are you in for?" I finally asked, half-joking like we were in prison to ease the tension.

"I am getting a liver transplant," she replied.

I almost started crying.

Ok, God, I thought.

"I had a liver transplant," I replied. I turned in my bed and looked across the IVs, the rail keeping us from rolling off, straight into her sweet eyes.

God, give me the words, I thought.

Just from the mention that I had what she was coming to receive – a liver transplant – everything in her spirit and body relaxed. I'm reminded of that quote from C.S. Lewis about friendship. He once wrote, "Friendship is born the moment that one person says to another, 'What? You too? I thought I was the only one!'"

Our connection was forged by the knowledge that I had traveled the unknown road before her and I lived to tell the tale. God moved in our midst that afternoon, and I spoke directly to her soul.

"You know God really loves you," I told her. "He thinks the world of you."

Tears filled her eyes. She nodded.

"Do you want to accept Jesus?" I asked her.

"Yes," she sputtered, through tears.

We prayed together and then cried. We sat there and cried, our anguish and suffering mingled with our Savior's grace. It was a glorious moment, and I dare say, much more rewarding than a week in Italy. The memory is made doubly sweet by the knowledge that she knew Jesus and is with Him today. She passed away a little over a month ago. Would I have enjoyed Italy? Sure. But, missing the trip was worth it. It was all worth it to be used by God just in time for someone who needed Him.

8

Regret and Reconciliation

I DON'T know where I heard this, or if I read it somewhere, but I think it's true: I don't believe that God is interested in worship nearly as much as He is interested in *worshipers*. Some of you might think that's heresy, but I think that's what God is looking for when Paul writes in Romans 12:1-2, "…present your bodies a living sacrifice, holy, acceptable to God, which is your *reasonable service.*"

The hard part of saying "yes" to God is accepting His reality that it's actually a reasonable service to be a living *sacrifice!* There are many opportunities along the way to abandon His call because the truth is it requires sacrifice to worship Him when life is difficult, when tragedy comes, or when we don't get our way.

My heart's desire is to worship Him in spirit and in truth. Even before I could give words to it, I have felt at home with the things of God. I longed to be near Him. From the time of my confirmation, I began attending Mass every morning before school. I knew that God was real, and I never doubted His power. I always desired His presence.

Though I knew who God was, and I was familiar with the liturgy and traditions of the church, I didn't accept Jesus as my Lord and Savior until I was an adult. It was 1975, and Gerry and I had been married for ten years. We attended a Marriage Encounter Retreat. We went not because we had a bad marriage but because we wanted to make our good marriage even better. The event was pivotal in our journey with God, and each other. The power of the Holy Spirit was so strong, during the final hours of the weekend if tongues of fire fell on all of our heads I wouldn't have been surprised. We came home more in love with each other and better able to communicate. It was an amazing time of intimacy and revelation. That weekend set us up for the next phase of our life together, as we learned what it meant to say "yes" to God.

At that time, the Charismatic Renewal Movement was in full swing throughout the Roman Catholic Church and I was drawn to the power of the Holy Spirit. I accepted Jesus into my life and became filled with the Holy Spirit. Some of the miracles that happened during these years are already covered in Chapter 1, but there was no shortage of the evidence of God's supernatural power during those days.

Maybe the 1970's were just a legitimately unique period, or maybe God was just working in my life in unique ways. Whichever, it was during this period that Gerry and I decided to sell everything we owned and live in voluntary poverty. When I say everything, I mean *everything*. We were committed to building a community of prayer that would honor God and be an example to others.

For a while, everything was glorious. God provided in amazing ways. From the simple things like food – I would often make a breakfast's worth of pancake batter on Monday, and it would last until Friday. It wasn't quite five loaves and two fish, but it was close!

We never lacked for anything. I had faith to move mountains. Looking back, I can honestly say it was easier to surrender and be generous when we had very little material wealth. The more we get, the harder it is to let go. I think being poor is easier than being rich.

As the prayer community launched, we had the blessing and support of the Catholic Church. We had a great priest who loved what was happening in our community. As things progressed, it became clear that many of the issues that caused the scandals of the past decade were rooted in an environment that protected the priests at the expense of the laity.

Though I don't personally believe that the leaders of the Catholic Church were systematically or even intentionally denying us an open forum for dialogue, the result of their priorities led to an environment that was destined to break down. As I learned the hard way, saying yes to God doesn't mean saying yes to everything a church leader asks or commands.

As time passed, it became clear that the priest in charge of our community was a narcissist. He lacked any leadership or even real vision for how we would advance in caring for people and loving God. He was seldom concerned with getting feedback from the rest of us. His lack of leadership created a very unhealthy environment. It was the absolute shirking of his duties that fostered a culture that allowed one of the other priests who was leading our community to lapse into full-blown alcoholism.

The alcoholic priest was partially responsible for the breakdown. Not only did he have unresolved personal issues, but we had genuine disagreements in theology. We didn't know him too well, and he was opposed to anything having to do with the Holy Spirit. Our lack of cohesiveness and his failure to lead appropriately started the downward spiral that ultimately brought an end to our community. Gerry and I met with our leadership and the Bishop about this, among other things.

I'LL NEVER FORGET the meeting Gerry and I had with the Bishop when the community was disbanding. It was a very painful time. I felt betrayed, isolated, and misunderstood. In spite of my fervent dedication to the community and sacrifice for God, I felt as though no one was listening to our concerns.

We met with the Bishop for over three hours. We told him everything from our perspective. Other members of the team were present, and it was as though our contention brought issues to the surface for everyone. There was incredible anger in the room. I could sense the great disappointment in God's heart for once again, men failed to love one another as He desires. Saying yes to God compelled us to say no to men who were abusive and arrogant and brought about tremendous strife. I did not believe our work was done. I did not believe the community was finished. I continued, even in the heated conversation, to believe that the community would find reconciliation and continue the work of God.

It was clear that it would take some time. It was clear that we were not going to continue as we had been. Even so, I believed in what we had done and what we could do. At one point in the discussion, I said, "Well, when the ministry starts back up again…"

The Bishop immediately cut me off. He jumped up and slammed his fists on the desk. His face reddened. Anger flashed in his eyes. He leaned across the desk and shouted, "There will be no ministry until there is forgiveness and there is repentance!"

It was a shot to the heart. He cut everything down in one fell swoop. As his words rang in my ears, the East Boston in me rose up. I refused to accept his words. Maybe it was the anger in his voice, or maybe it was the statement itself. Whichever, or both, it triggered ferocity in me. It provoked my stubborn streak and I gave in to my flesh. My response to his declaration was one of the biggest mistakes I've ever made. In that moment I hardened my heart. I thought to myself, *who the hell is he to tell me to forgive and repent?"*

IN SOME RESPECTS, I was completely within my rights to feel that way. After everything we'd done, at the end of over three years of serving and sacrificing and working to build the community of prayer, it all fell apart. After all that, when the meeting with the Bishop concluded, he simply thanked us for coming and told us good-bye. He didn't console us. He didn't pacify us. He very calmly and professionally thanked us for coming, as though we had just given a presentation on carpet samples for the parish.

In spite of our conversation, nothing changed. The alcoholic priest who was part of our group was merely re-assigned. No one said a word to us after that day. It was as though the last few years of our life had just been thrown away. Not only that, but it was as though our voice was meaningless. My anger rose in defense of all the people like me who I knew went unheard. My anger rose in support of the discouragement I felt. And so, I allowed the bitterness to fester, and fester it did. The grudge I held spread like a virus and infected my mind and my body. Dr. James Dobson says, "The mind, body and soul are close neighbors, and one usually inherits the ills of the other." After the experience I had with my unforgiveness, I know it to be true.

From the day I walked out of the Bishop's office, and every day for the next two years, I got sicker and sicker. My body endured one illness after another that ultimately led to the surgical removal of my colon. My anger and bitterness literally ate away at my insides. All I did during that time was find and talk with people who had also been offended by the Catholic Church. We would get together and murmur and complain and sow discord. All we were doing was feeding each other's self-pity and feeding the disease of holding grudges within our bodies and souls.

SOME YEARS LATER, I attended the Leanne Payne School of Pastoral Care. It was a week-long intensive seminar on healing from relational brokenness. It was a remarkable experience full of personal growth and awareness. My past was littered with brokenness caused by dysfunctional family members, my own insecurities and sins, and an inability to see myself as God saw me – lovely and lovable.

While writing this book, Leanne Payne went home to be with Jesus. Her work had a significant influence in my life. I have always greatly admired Leanne Payne. She held an important balance between the Word and the Spirit in her ministry. I often compared her writings with C.S. Lewis. And, I would use much of what I learned from her in my own teachings.

In many ways, I considered her to be a mentor. Attending her school of Pastoral Care was one of the most cherished and healing times of my life. The one thing that I remember most from my time under her leadership was that she had not "techniques" or "methods" for pastoral prayer. It was simply open obedience and surrender to God. I remember most of all that I got closer to Jesus. There were no "special prayers" but the presence of Jesus was real and true.

I didn't know much of her personal life but I am sure she learned through her personal experiences. I have a tremendous admiration for her. When she passed I think we lost someone precious to us, but greatly loved by God.

When I attended the week of intensive seminars, I was there to develop skills and be trained in helping others overcome relational brokenness. Of course, as is often the case, I went thinking I was receiving training, and ended up receiving healing for my own life. The week was spent in learning but also developing an understanding for my own experience. A major relational brokenness that I uncovered was my relationship with the Catholic Church.

In addition to the experience I described earlier, with the alcoholic priest and the Bishop, my own family had endured sexual abuse from priests. As I was in the environment of healing and prayerful restoration, God prepared my heart to fully experience the kind of restoration I doubted was ever possible.

In the week-long seminar, we were encouraged to be transparent with those around us. I ended up sharing meals and time with a group of people that included a Catholic priest. True to myself, I didn't hold back. I shared openly what I'd experienced.

At the end of the week, in the middle of worship, the same priest with whom I'd shared meals and details of my painful experience with the church tapped me on the shoulder. I turned, as the voices of everyone around me sang freely in adoration to God. The priest's clear voice cut through all the singing. What he said split my heart wide open. His words drilled right to the core of the brokenness:

"I want to stand in the gap for everyone who isn't here – for everyone who harmed you – I want to ask for you to forgive the Catholic Church. Will you forgive us?"

I collapsed into his open arms; my full weight leaned into his chest. He steadied himself and held me, as my racking sobs shook us both and my streaming tears stained his shirt. For the next twenty minutes, I released all the pain and hurt I'd stored up. It was the most cathartic experience of my life. With each tear that fell, a piece of the shell I'd build up around my heart crumbled away. In that moment, I understood the love that God has for us and the incredible desire He has for us to love one another.

I realized that though I never left the church out of anger, I did lose my affection for the Catholic Church. Though I was responsible for the bitterness I'd allowed to grow in my heart, as I felt God's healing in that seminar, I also received His revelation. He was simply calling me to something different when the Bishop closed the community. I misread the situation and allowed the human interaction to taint my thinking. If it hadn't happened, I may never have been able to be used by God in the way He intended.

From time to time, even though it had not returned, I still felt nostalgia for the way things had been before – the way I'd loved Mass as a teenager. I appreciated the symbolism, the tradition, and the heritage of the Catholic Church. Though I disagree with some of the church's teaching, I honor what God has done through it and in my own life as a formation of my faith.

MORE THAN A DECADE after I'd experienced God's healing at the Leanne Payne seminar, I was invited to join a group with the International Prayer Organization. We were invited to go to Italy to pray. I was honored to be included, as this gathering brought together significant intercessors from around the world. People came from Egypt, England, Switzerland, and Finland, just to name a few. These were influential people who pray with an expectation of incredible moves of God. We were like Special Forces or Navy SEALs in the realm of prayer and intercession.

The presence of the Holy Spirit was palpable. I knew God was in our midst and I was excited about what I was sure would come about as a result of our intercessory prayer. I was also very excited about the opportunity to pray at St. Peter's Square in Rome. Not only that, but the retreat center where we stayed was beautiful. I could walk on the roof and see the entire city. It was breathtaking. I could imagine the apostle Paul coming to meet Caesar. I imagined St. Peter himself, evangelizing the locals before being condemned to die.

The day came for us to go into Rome and pray. As we gathered at St. Peter's Square, one of the intercessors, a man from England, expressed nervousness about praying. He said there were too many spirits in the air. At first, we tried to pacify him. We tried to encourage him that we should pray, but he was insistent. Such was the force of his desire to avoid praying there, we finally relented. We returned to the retreat center to pray.

We began praying fervently in a room in the retreat center. As we stood interceding, I asked God for specific guidance as to my prayer.

"I want you to continue to forgive and bless the church," He whispered.

For the two years before this moment, I had been working to purposely forgive the Catholic church and priests whenever I saw either. As God spoke that day, I didn't hesitate. I didn't pause.

"Yes, God. Yes!" I fell on the floor, and the words flowed like a rushing river. "I forgive the church. Lord, bless the church," I cried. "Pour out your blessing and favor upon the church, dear Lord," I prayed, as tears flooded the ground beneath me.

As I prayed, through tightly shut eyes, I saw flashes of light. In between the flashes of light, I saw a vision of thousands upon thousands of people streaming into the Kingdom of God through the work of the Catholic Church. I was overwhelmed by what I saw. I was overcome by what I felt. The power of the Holy Spirit was unleashed in the room.

As I continued to pray, to forgive, and to bless, the man who didn't want to pray in St. Peter's Square remarked, "Do you see those flashes of light?!"

"Yes, I see them," I said.

We rejoiced in the presence of God that day. The sky became filled with a lightning storm. Thunder cracked and hail began to fall. The air was electric and the sky looked like a storm that might have been written about in the book of Revelation.

In my immediate surrender to God's request, I experienced a personal revelation. I understood the power of saying yes to God. Saying yes to God releases the power of the Holy Spirit for the Kingdom. As the power of nature was released in the sky all around us, I felt like the power of the Holy Spirit was released in my instant obedience to God's request that I forgive the Church. As we observed and felt the power of God's Creation, I understood the importance of my own life and my willingness to say "yes" to Him.

"Do you know why I have been able to use you for so many extraordinary experiences?" God asked me.

Before I could reply, He answered His own question.

"Because I know you'll say 'yes.' Because I know you'll say 'yes' without hesitation," He finished. I could feel Him smiling at me, a proud Father looking at his little girl.

I know that God has used me, in however and for whomever He has willed, because I say yes to Him. I say yes when it's easy, I say yes when it's hard. I say yes when things are well, I say yes when life feels like hell on earth. No matter what, no matter when, I say "yes" to God. This attribute, above all else, releases God's power, through His Holy Spirit.

I CHANGED MY LANGUAGE. After that night in Italy, with the sky erupting in a wonderful thunderstorm, I continued speaking blessings toward the Catholic Church. It was a daily exercise. God made it easy, by reminding me to keep saying yes to forgiveness. Every time I felt unforgiveness rise in my heart, I would arrest it and speak forgiveness.

I began to stop thinking about the negative experiences and chose to focus on the blessings and miracles I'd witnessed by saying "yes" to God. I have regrets, but I've learned that even the regrets can be rewards when you are willing to accept that all of it – the sorrow, the anger, the pain – is worked out by God for our ultimate good, if we are willing to say yes to Him.

My faith journey has been ecumenical, maybe even eclectic. From Roman Catholic confirmation as a child to communal living to Assemblies of God to an ordained Anglican priest, I've learned to love worshiping God in a variety of expressions and liturgies.

Regardless of the form or tradition, I have found that saying yes to God requires humility, vision and sacrifice. I learned this well during an experience at an Assemblies of God church in 2005 and earlier, during my experience building the Connecticut House of Prayer.

One day in 2005, during my morning prayer, I started singing an old hymn.

What can wash away my sins? Nothing but the blood of Jesus,
What can make me whole again? Nothing but the blood of Jesus.

This was very unusual for me. It was a really great prayer time. God was speaking to me and I felt the presence of the Lord. You ever have one of those times where you go from happy to sad in a moment? Nothing changed in the environment, but something changed in my spirit. Like a switch was flipped. It doesn't make sense, but that's kind of what happened to me that morning.

After that wonderful moment, as I walked into the kitchen, for some reason I went from rejoicing in the Lord to deciding I couldn't continue to be involved in ministry. It was a Sunday morning and it was as though during my walk from my prayer chair, through the living room and into the kitchen, every step stripped away another piece of my joy. By the time I reached the kitchen, where Gerry was fixing breakfast, I decided I was through. I allowed thoughts about difficult things and general frustrations to put me in a funk. You ever have those kinds of days? It almost feels good to be in a bad mood, you know what I mean? I allowed the difficulties I'd been dealing with to get into my head and I was convinced that I'd had enough.

"I'm quitting," I said as I walked through the doorway.

"You're quitting what?" Gerry replied.

"Church. I'm done helping them. I am done doing so much. Nobody notices or cares anyway."

"But, we were going to try the church that you mentioned a couple weeks ago. It sounds really great."

"Forget it," I grumped. "I'm done."

Gerry looked at me. "I really don't think that's the case. But I suppose if you are going to stop helping, you should at least tell them. The service is starting soon. You still want to go?"

Gerry is so funny that way. He didn't put up a big fuss. He didn't try to correct me or condemn me for my desire to quit. He knew that God would work it out – He always does.

So, we went to church, a few minutes late. As our family piled through the back door of the sanctuary, Gerry was walking Gretchen in slowly, Philip was waving and smiling at everyone, and I was silently sulking. I was in rare form. Every mile we drove to get there, my heart grew more and more upset with all the work I'd done without appreciation. I felt like I was getting the silent treatment from God. That's the way it goes when you say yes to God. He doesn't always respond the way we want. But He always comes along at the right moment to make sure we keep pursuing Him.

Wouldn't you know it, as we walked into the service, the congregation was singing an old hymn.

"What can wash away my sins? Nothing but the blood of Jesus."

I smiled a little bit and kind of nodded to God. *Ok,* I thought, *good one, God.* The very hymn that I'd been singing that morning, which was unusual, was being sung in a contemporary Assemblies of God service, again very unusual.

We joined in the worship and as I sang, it was with a reluctant heart. My mouth and lungs pushed out the words, but my heart and mind were thinking about some ways I'd been offended by people in the church. I was ticked. I was not going to let God move me just by the coincidence of the song we were singing being the same as the one I'd sung that morning!

After worship, we sat down and the pastor began to speak.

"In between services, I often go into my office to pray," he said. "Depending on the day, I'll ask God for wisdom or strength or to let me know if there's someone who needs encouragement."

The congregation sat attentively listening. I sat aggravated and fuming as the pastor continued to speak.

"God didn't say anything to me, but when I walked out of my office, I looked and there, right in my line of sight was Barbara Lachance. There she is," the pastor pointed directly to me in front of the whole church, "I want to thank Barbara Lachance. All these years, you have been faithful and served the people of God in the state of Connecticut. Thank you. You are a wonderful blessing to the Kingdom of God."

In that moment, it all melted away – my offense, my anger, my disappointment. I truly had labored for many years and I believed that no one noticed. As I was on the verge of quitting once again, God spoke through our pastor directly to my heart. God whispered, "I see you, Barbara. I know what you have given to Me, and I know what you have *given up* for Me."

ABOUT SIX YEARS BEFORE that re-affirming moment, I experienced a tremendous year of saying yes to God. Saying yes to God has taken me on many paths, but throughout the work of the church, nothing has been as challenging and fulfilling as building the Connecticut House of Prayer.

I had recently resigned my position at Vineyard Christian Fellowship (I told you I had a wide variety of experiences in church), and I didn't know what to do. I've never been one who is good at sitting still. I need to be doing something, but at the time I was physically exhausted. So, I told God to make me an intercessor. I didn't ask Him, mind you. I told Him, which always ends up getting me in a crazy place!

Of course, after I told Him to make me an intercessor, I had no idea what I was getting into. But, I'd decided to be an intercessor, so every morning I went out onto our porch to soak up the sun and to be soaked by the Son. I wrote in my journal and asked God to show me what was next for my life.

It had been an abrupt transition for me. I went from working 65 hours per week to doing what seemed like nothing. I wasn't exactly doing nothing, because I was still caring for my family, but I was no longer active in ministry. Though I tried to get involved in different areas, nothing seemed to work out. It felt like God had put me in a closet and was waiting for me to settle down before He would allow me to do anything.

I recall reading a great story once about St. Therese of Lisieux. As I remember, she said something like this: "If I am the play thing of the child Jesus and He desires to put me in a corner to collect dust, that is fine. Who am I to complain?"

What a difficult thing to say. What a powerful testimony. When we reach the point where we desire only to be in the place He desires us to be, I believe we are completely able to say yes to God.

My stubborn spirit did not enjoy the seclusion, but I had asked to be an intercessor. Or, more to the point, I *told* God to make me one. Like I said, I tend to speak my mind, even when my mind hasn't really thought things through.

After I got into the rhythms of my new season of life, an opportunity presented itself in the form of the Strategic Prayer Network. The Strategic Prayer Network was a regional and national assembly of people from all over America, who were dedicated to intercessory prayer. Started in Colorado Springs by Cindy Jacobs, the Strategic Prayer Network soon had state leaders and groups praying all over the nation, for our nation.

Before too long I became the Connecticut state coordinator for the Strategic Prayer Network. I tried to combine my declaration of becoming an intercessor with my inability to sit still. Believe it or not, God was able to do it. During a visit to Colorado, I saw the World Prayer Center and became convinced that the state of Connecticut needed something similar. I returned home and started sharing the vision for the Connecticut House of Prayer with several pastor friends.

After a considerable time of prayer, we came into a financial windfall. Gerry received an unexpected significant bonus and he decided to give it to me to help begin the ministry. By March 1999, we had a dedication service and life really took off. My original thought was that we would establish a 24/7 House of Prayer but God had other ideas. As I started networking and spreading the word about what we were doing, I discovered that I really had a gift for connecting with people. I made friendships everywhere I went. God gave me favor with many people, and before long I was invited to coordinate a Promise Keepers event at the Hartford Civic Center. I was asked to set up the schedule for the event, and build a team of intercessors who helped to spread the word about the event. Every time, God brought amazing people in to help me, people who had a heart to work, and a passion for saying yes to God. No matter what anyone says, nothing great happens without lots of sacrificial effort.

It was a lot of work, and though I was often worn out, God refreshed me. When the night came and I saw men streaming to the floor from every corner of the arena to accept Jesus, I was moved to tears.

After that, I was asked to coordinate prayer for the Louis Palau Festivals that were happening all over the state of Connecticut. That year, I drove forty-five thousand miles all over the state! It was an amazing time. We built a group of 1,700 intercessors. The Louis Palau Festivals were successful in building great unity in our state. Over the course of the year, we raised two and a half million dollars for the festivals, but it didn't yield the kind of salvation response I anticipated. There was little visible result in the churches, but something happened in the spiritual realm. Prayer became commonplace throughout the state. We held our first statewide pastors gathering and 175 leaders came. From that first year, God has continued to bless prayer throughout Connecticut, and the influence of that organization continues to this day.

The beauty of this experience was I learned that prayer transcends denominations and cultures in a way nothing else can. During our meetings, we had a diversity that I believe reflects the heart of God. One friend of mine, an evangelical leader in his own church, approached me after a prayer gathering of nearly 4,500 people at the Hartford Civic Center. He was clearly moved and inspired. The Holy Spirit was at work, and I was so blessed by his remarks.

"I heard people speaking in Spanish, some in English, and some in tongues, but it all sounded like angels."

It was like Pentecost all over again. The power of prayer is underestimated by almost everyone, including me. Reminders of moments like this are important to return the focus to what really matters.

My involvement in the prayer movement has taken me around the world. It has deepened my faith and it has pulled down strongholds. I've witnessed a state transformed in the spiritual realm, and I've experienced real miracles. It has been a great privilege and blessing, and I'm forever grateful I said "yes" to God. Or more appropriately in this case, that He said "yes" to me.

9

The Dark Night of the Soul

I've been to five different doctors this week. As I write this chapter, I realize that some people might think I'm exaggerating the severity and frequency of the illnesses I've endured over the past thirty years. As crazy as it sounds, it's all true. For over three decades, my body has been ravaged by ailments that have brought about extended hospital stays and invasive surgeries. Some have brought me to the brink of death, yet I remain here. I remain ready to say yes to God.

There is a point in human existence where the body lives only because the spirit fights. I know this place well. There is an expression I've discovered which defines this place. The moment you hear it, if you've spent time in this place you know that this phrase is right on. It's The Dark Night of The Soul.

The Dark Night of the Soul is actually the title of a poem written by a 16th century Spanish poet and Roman Catholic mystic named Saint John of the Cross. That term, which is the title of this chapter, has taken on a meaning of its own. It is used to describe a period of spiritual crisis or darkness through which a person may grow closer to God.

Many writers believe that Mother Teresa experienced this for nearly fifty years, with only mild and occasional relief from the darkness. Saint Therese of Lisieux wrote of the darkness that she was "plunged into." This darkness can take many forms. For some, it's an emotional or psychological debilitation like depression or fear. For others, like me, it's a physical impairment. It can become so difficult and persistent that hope begins to wane. Yet, I know that God has a plan. I refuse to believe that He can't heal. I refuse to believe that His love is somehow lesser toward me because I don't have perfect health.

As I mentioned in Chapter 1, the question "why?" sometimes sneaks into my mind. Sometimes, it shouts from my heart. I've had half my insides removed. The hospital janitor knows me by name. The condition of my body is not what I envisioned for my life. There are days when I've told God, "Either kill me or heal me, just make up your mind!" It's easy to begin wondering if I did something wrong. It's easy to believe that somehow, someway, I deserve this incredible hardship.

I have tried everything known to Christianity to alleviate my pain. I've been prayed over by some of the most renowned faith healers in the world. I've gone through deliverance, generational curses, soaking prayer, and healing prayer. I've been anointed with oil. I've read books, listened to sermons, and prayed through the night. (The nurses wake me up every hour to give me medicine, so it wasn't like I was sleeping anyway.)

At some point along the journey, I realized that God never promised a life of perfect health. And even though I've seen many people completely healed, it hasn't yet happened for me. I realized that saying yes to God required me to accept that what Jesus told the disciples was also for me. It's for all of us. The passage I'm referring to is found in Mark 10:29-31. It's a wonderful promise, but it contains a clause that makes it difficult for those who choose to proclaim the gospel. Here's the passage in its entirety:

> "Truly I tell you," Jesus replied, "no one who has left home or brothers or sisters or mother or father or children or fields for me and the gospel will fail to receive a hundred times as much in this present age: homes, brothers, sisters, mothers, children and fields – *along with persecutions* – and in the age to come eternal life. But many who are first will be last, and the last first.

What a great promise! Jesus knows – in fact, he's responding to Peter saying that he'd left everything to follow – all the sacrifices we make to follow Him. And He tells the disciples, and us, that we will receive everything we've left and then some. Sounds wonderful! Yet, in the middle of it, He interjects that there will be persecutions. It's almost like an aside, like an afterthought. It's sort of an "Oh, by the way, fellas" moment.

So, we have all these blessings, but they come with persecutions. I hate the *P* word! The word persecution appears in the New Testament nine times[12], and eight of them identify persecution as attendant to the spread of the gospel, or preaching about Jesus Christ, specifically. The remaining verse, Romans 8:35, tells us that persecution, among other things, cannot separate us from the love of Christ.

While I am not saying that my illness has been a direct attack from the enemy, it is clear that suffering and persecution often effect those who are spreading the Gospel, which I have done and will always do. I am not one to blame illness on spiritual attack. I do believe that we can contribute to our illnesses and diseases by not caring for our bodies. A good example would be someone who gets lung cancer after smoking for several decades.

In my case, there were likely things I could have done better to take care of my physical health. My diet, my activities, my personal habits; all could have contributed to providing a place for illness to grow. I do believe we can make choices that provide the enemy with fertile ground to attack us. Please don't misunderstand me. I'm not saying that you can make all the right choices and you'll avoid sickness. The human body exists in a fallen world, and in a degenerative state. But, we can do better to keep ourselves unspotted from the world, and perhaps limit our sufferings. But, make no mistake, persecution will come. It's a promise, in Mark 10, as I mentioned just a few pages earlier.

As I reflect on my life, I see the truth of this promise. I have a wonderful home, a great family, and financial provisions. I have fields. Real fields. We live on a beautiful farm with rolling hills and wide-open spaces. It's everything anyone could want in this temporary life on earth. Yet, I have battled sickness for most of my adult life. The blessings of my life are far greater than the terrible physical suffering I've endured. Even when going through severe pain, I say, "Thank you, God." Even while my back is killing me, I remember that worship kills the devil. God's blessings always overshadow the darkness we may go through. Reconciling this paradox is the journey through my Dark Night of the Soul.

ALONG THE WAY, I've learned a few things. The greatest lesson of all is the power of gratitude. Thankfulness is the virtue that carries me through it all. Gratitude is the elixir that lifts my spirit when my body falls down. Giving thanks in the ordinary things, and doing it daily, has been my saving grace. I have learned that when I focus on the day I'm living in, and focus on being grateful for the little things that we so often take for granted, I receive God's "peace that passes all understanding."[13] It goes beyond my natural mind, which is why it can't be understood. Yet, in the midst of the storm, there is contentment in my spirit because I remain thankful for the blessings in my life.

It reminds me of the story of Jesus asleep in the storm. In Matthew 8, we read of the disciples in a boat with Jesus. They were crossing the sea to visit the region of the Gadarenes, where two demon-possessed men awaited. Once they got over, Jesus performed an amazing miracle by casting the demons out of the men, for the Bible describes the demon-possessed men as being "so violent that no one could pass that way."[14]

Before Jesus could bring the supernatural deliverance to the two men, and while He and the disciples were still crossing the sea, "a furious storm came up on the lake, so that the waves swept over the boat."[15]

The disciples started freaking out. Remember, some of the disciples were experienced fishermen. They were used to the wind and waves. No doubt some of them had spent most of their lives on the open water. Yet this furious storm was so powerful that they cried out, "We're going to drown!"[16]

Meanwhile, Jesus was in the lower part of the boat, sound asleep. While the surge threatened to take the boat down, and all the men with it, Jesus was catching up on his rest. The disciples, filled with fear, shouted for His help and woke Him up. Many are the times we see a storm coming, or find ourselves in the middle of a tempest, and shout to God – "Hey, where are you? Wake up! I'm dying here!"

Jesus, of course, woke up. Did He freak out? No. Did He tell the disciples to abandon ship? No. Jesus, as always, brought perspective. He brought power. He brought peace. His response to the disciples was straightforward and strong. "You of little faith, why are you so afraid?"[17] He asked. Then He rebuked the storm and it was *completely calm.*

Jesus. He brought the disciples through the storm without any big show or flowery speech. He just spoke and everything was completely calm. I find that when I am grateful instead of fearful, I see the world as Jesus does. Like the disciples, if I focus on the danger of the storm, I start to shout from fright. I start to doubt the very One who brought me into the boat. But if I focus on the great things Jesus is doing, and if I realize that on the other side of the storm is a mighty miracle, I become completely calm. Either way, Jesus will show up, but if I keep my heart full of gratitude, I don't have to be scolded by Him. I don't have to hear Him say, "You of little faith, why are you so afraid?"

AS I WROTE ABOVE, Jesus brings perspective. Most often, I've found that He brings perspective through the people He brings into our lives. For me, that perspective often comes through ministering to others even when I don't feel like it. Recently, I was going through a frustrating period. I wanted to feel sorry for myself, and I kind of doubted what I was even doing. I was scheduled to go to speak at a healing meeting. Yet, I have been sick so often. I was thinking, am I even qualified to speak? I'm not totally healed. The usual doubts of not being worthy – like Moses, Gideon, and Ruth, virtually everyone God's ever used – crept into my mind.

To top it off, as I was driving to the meeting, I ended up taking a wrong turn, and drove about twenty minutes out of the way. Now, I was probably going to be late. Why even go? Maybe the wrong turn was meant to be. Maybe I should just go home? All the excuses that we use when we don't feel like doing what God wants us to do started popping into my head.

For some reason, I ignored those excuses. Again, I said yes to God a long time ago, and I have learned that more often than not, saying yes to God will lead me in a direction my flesh doesn't want to go. So, I went. I said yes to God once again. And, once again, I'm very glad I did. This time, the perspective that came humbled me and reminded me that on the other side of my "yes, God" is someone else's "please, God."

As I entered the church and waited to be introduced, I still had some residual selfish "poor me" attitude in my heart. Then, the pastor got up and she said, "The Reverend Barbara Lachance is here. She's going to be teaching us today. She's going to help us today." As she spoke, the pastor began crying. With tears streaming down her face (and egg all over mine – I felt about two feet tall as I realized how selfish I'd been), she talked about how excited they were for me to come speak with them. You would have thought I was the Queen of England or some famous movie star, the way she went on and on.

She continued introducing me, but she turned to me directly and said, "Barbara, I know the work God is calling you to. We want you to come here and be blessed, and we appreciate your service and your gifts. When you go out from here, we bless you and are supportive of all that God is doing through your life."

I nearly broke down. Not only did she give me a glowing introduction, she affirmed all that I was doing. She wasn't selfish. She was eager to learn, and the room was full of people who were eager to grow. And God had chosen to use me to help them grow! Ten minutes earlier, I was questioning even showing up. I was feeling bad for myself, and as a result, I almost missed the opportunity to participate in a miracle. Once again,

Jesus brought me perspective, and a gentle reminder. Once again, like He did with the disciples in the storm, He looked at me and asked me, "Where is your faith?"

My faith remains in Him. But only when I focus on remaining grateful, only when I focus on the miracle on the other side of the storm, can I be completely calm. Then the peace that passes all understanding floods my soul and I see past the pain and suffering. The Dark Night of the Soul is no easy stretch, and persecution is not fun. But, saying yes to God is the only way to not just survive the Dark Night of the Soul, but to see His power through it all and to feel His peace in the middle of it all.

10

Loving the Unloved

NONE OF OUR CHILDREN, biological or adopted, ever really expressed curiosity about why our family took in so many of society's outcasts. For nearly two decades, we always had an assortment of developmentally disabled people, of all ages, living in our home. There was nothing typical about our family environment, but I don't think there's anything typical about God's love. The Bible has many stories about the importance, even the godliness, of caring for those who can't care for themselves. Every day, our family loved the unloved, and as a result, our children learned to do the same.

Throughout the years of loving the unloved, we learned that they were just as human as anyone. They felt pain, they desired affirmation. They enjoyed laughter. Throughout the years, we also learned that there are plenty of people who, through ignorance, arrogance, or fear, mistreated the unloved in ways that are more than mere embarrassment.

The following stories contain humor, tragedy, and achievement. Much like every life, the lives of disabled people contain a variety of experiences that define their days. These stories are all true, from my biological children's memories. I hope they remind you that we are all flawed in some way. We all need God's grace. I hope they inspire you to enter into a conversation with someone who has disabilities. I hope they inspire you to love the unloved.

Allen "Moose". (as remembered by Paul Lachance)

Allen "Moose" was a foster brother to me. He was one of the youngest people who came to live with us in the early days of the group home. He was severely mentally retarded. He was a smaller guy, but strong and actually quite athletic. Like a lot of Down's Syndrome kids, Allen was genuinely and consistently happy. He was always smiling, and as a result, I smiled when I was with him.

He enjoyed life. It was the late 1970's and early 1980's, and he was a fanatic of the Muppets. He loved the first generation of Muppet movies. To this day, every time I hear the "Rainbow Connection" song made famous by Kermit the Frog, I think of Allen. You know the song with the lines, "Some day we'll find it, a rainbow connection, the lovers, the dreamers, and me...". He used to hum along loudly, every time it came on the TV.

I smile thinking of it today, over thirty years later. I can picture him, sitting there with a big grin, humming along with Kermit. The differences between us were far fewer than the commonalities. When we watched the Muppets, or did our secret handshake, we were just two boys having fun.

Living in New England left us no choice but to be Red Sox fans. And Allen would get very excited whenever I'd ask him, "Allen, who is your favorite baseball player?"

He'd start grinning.

I'd prompt him by softly sounding out, "Doooooo..."

"Doooo," he would repeat. Then he would finish the name loudly and sometimes with a clap, "Dewey Evans!"

He was quirky. He had idiosyncrasies, like all of us. One of the most exasperating quirks (at least to me) he had was his eating habits. No matter what the food was; Swedish meatballs, macaroni and cheese, lima beans, etc., he would never eat more than one piece at a time. I'd be sitting next to him at dinner and he would place one lima bean on his fork and eat it. Then he'd place one Swedish meatball on his fork and eat it. Never would he allow more than one of any food item to be on his fork or in his mouth. Mealtime with Allen took forever!

Breakfast cereal was the worst. One morning, I got so frustrated by watching how long it took Allen to eat his Cheerios, I grabbed his wrist and pushed his spoon into the bowl. I held onto his wrist and pulled it back up toward his mouth. Drops of milk ran down the handle, spilling onto the kitchen table. No less than ten Cheerios sat in the spoon, swimming in the milk, ready to be eaten in a single bite. Or so, I hoped.

I let go of Allen's wrist and leaned back in my seat. I was a teenager at the time, and I can only speculate, but I guess I thought I was helping him. I was doing what almost all of us "normal" people do. I was transferring my way of doing something, and the way most people did something, onto

Allen. Perhaps it was my subconscious mind directing me to "help" him be like everyone else. What I learned through sharing life with Allen, and dozens of other developmentally disabled people, was that he didn't really want to be "helped" in that way.

He held the spoon aloft, hovering near his full lips. I sat up straight with anticipation. Allen was going to eat the whole spoonful. This might seem like a little thing, but you have no idea how long mealtime was with him. The efficiency I was bringing to his life was akin to the invention of the combustion engine!

He looked over the spoon full of Cheerios, straight into my eyes. He grinned.

He gets it, I thought.

"Go ahead, Allen, eat it," I said.

He pulled it closer to his mouth and paused.

"Come on," I urged.

Closer and closer, he inched the spoon to his mouth until it was almost touching his lips. Then he smiled even bigger, as he extended his lips and picked off one, solitary Cheerio. He pulled it into his mouth and crunched it loudly. He continued, picking one Cheerio at a time, into his mouth until the entire spoon was empty.

He returned the spoon to the bowl and began laughing.

And so did I.

David. (as remembered by Tracy Lachance)

David was an easy-going kid. He was eager to laugh, and eager to please. He, like many of the younger people who came to live with us, hadn't been de-humanized by decades of institutional care. He got excited about celebrations, and one of the best moments in my memory came during the time we celebrated his birthday.

As always, Mom had prepared a wonderful cake — she always believed in honoring everyone as often as possible — for David's birthday. All we had to do was finish our dinner, and it would be time for a rich, six-layered red velvet cake. Six layers of moist cake and delicious homemade frosting. Six layers of heaven! Most of us kids had been eyeing it all afternoon, waiting for the moment that was now just moments away.

We'd finished our dinner, and as we sat around the table, Mom went into the kitchen to place candles on the cake, light them, and return to the festivities. As Mom disappeared into the kitchen, David reached out and grabbed half a carrot from the remnants of food on his plate. He shoved it in his mouth and started chomping away.

At the moment, I thought nothing of it. All I could think about was the cake. Around the table, each child was grinning expectantly. Funny how such simple pleasures can be so fulfilling for everyone while young. Yet, many allow the hardships of life to grind them down over time, until joy is all but gone. As Mom wrote earlier, one of the beauties of the developmentally disabled is the incredible joy they express over the simple wonders of life. I wonder, who was really being helped when we cared for them?

"Happy birthday to you, happy birthday to you," the chorus rang out from around the table as Mom entered, a massive cake draped in fresh buttercream frosting in her arms. Candles were glowing, and anticipation was at a fever pitch.

"Happy birthday dear David, happy birthday to you!"

"Now make a wish," someone yelled out, as Mom set the cake right in front of David.

I don't know if Mom noticed, but us kids did. As we finished the song, David was still chomping on carrot, mixing the whole orange mess with saliva, like a puree machine in his mouth.

"Ok, dear," Mom encouraged. "You can blow out the candles."

David was a good boy. He bent forward, mouth still full of carrot, took a deep breath and blew – make that sprayed – the entire cake, table and anything within ten feet of his mouth, with shredded carrot.

Everyone stared, unsure of what to do. The cake! It was covered in carrot shreds, and David's spit.

"We can still eat it," Mom said. Without a fuss or fume, Mom picked up the cake and returned to the kitchen. She came back moments later, with a delicious five-layer red velvet cake.

Everyone laughed. And everyone ate.

This is one of our favorite memories because it demonstrates the unexpected events of life with developmentally disabled people, and the can-do attitude Mom carried into every moment. She never lost her cool. If something was an honest mistake, Mom just rolled along, and we all had a great time as a result.

Carey. (as remembered by Tracy Lachance)

Not every memory is laughter and silly, fun exchanges. Life with those who have severe mental deficiencies and major physical disabilities is complicated, challenging and selfless. But it's worth it. No one can help everyone but we can all help someone. And that's really the essence of loving the unloved.

When the state hospital was closed, people were actually being released into the streets. There were some people who had been in custodial care for years, and were released without any place to go. One of those people was Carey. Carey was a grown man who had likely never experienced much compassion or even real personal interaction with other people in any meaningful way.

Carey was a severe case. His behavior really showed the de-humanizing effect of institutionalizing people with mental disabilities. They became prisoners. Really, in many ways, they became like animals. Carey was one of them. He played with feces, he regurgitated his food. He bit people. He was ornery and strong and difficult.

One day, I stayed home from school. Either I wasn't feeling well, or I just needed a break. Mom never pushed us to go to school when we were genuinely sick or run down. She knew life was much more than school work, though she is an absolute believer and advocate of education; she had a balance with us that makes me forever grateful.

Anyway, on that day I stayed home, I was sitting on my mother's lap watching *Guiding Light*. Talk about education! The issues those characters dealt with were something else.

For some reason, Carey was on the floor, between my line of sight and the TV. He was rocking back and forth, a very common tic developed by people with developmental disabilities.

"Carey, please move," I asked.

He didn't respond. He just kept rocking.

"Come on Carey, can you please move?" I asked again.

Again, he didn't respond.

"Carey, did you hear me? Please move. I can't see the TV."

The third time was the charm, sort of. He did move, but then he walked up to me and whacked me on the back like he was smacking a stubborn donkey that wouldn't move.

It knocked the wind out of me. I started crying and screaming.

Mom jumped up and sent Carey out of the room before tending to me. I recovered, but that moment remains a terrible memory for me.

After that, Carey had to go to another home. Mom and Dad were full of compassion but they weren't going to allow their children to be endangered.

It was too bad. As I think about it now, as a grown woman, I have context. I think about the experiences of Carey's life. I have no idea what was done to him, or how he suffered during his years in institutional care.

Of course, he couldn't remain with us, which is the sad part. We couldn't help Carey. And yet, he's a person just like me. The effect of isolation and limitations in his life were severe and devastating.

I think it's a shame that more people aren't exposed to those who have developmental disabilities. All the time, I remember people just staring at our family. Because Mom and Dad brought everyone along, whether it was a grocery store or a restaurant, or vacation, we'd walk in with five or six developmentally disabled people, and the reaction from others was the same as if we'd walk in with a bunch of three-headed green aliens from outer space.

It's not like the developmentally disabled asked to be that way. They are human beings. Most people just have never been exposed to them. It's a shame because all of us "normal" people could learn a lot from the innocence, strength, and hopefulness of the people I grew up with. The people I call friend, brother, sister.

Once I was waiting tables, and a lady entered with a small group of people with special needs. I got so excited.

"That table is mine," I said.

I rushed over and took their drink orders. As I did, I recognized one of the girls as someone who'd lived with us for a little while. I couldn't remember her name, as I had been little and she hadn't lived with us for very long.

"Do any of you know Philip Lachance?" I asked.

That girl got so excited. "Oh yes, oh yes, I know Philip," she said.

It was such a beautiful connection. We chatted briefly, and I walked away reminded of the simple joy that can be had when two people, regardless of labels or disabilities, just enjoy life and the blessing of being able to call another person, "friend."

Institutionalization of the Developmentally Disabled. (Paul Lachance)

As the oldest of my parent's biological children, I have a perspective on life with developmentally disabled people that may differ from my sister Tracy. I don't mean that we have a different approach to them – we both love them fully and equally. What I mean is I have memories of life before they came into mine. I have some sense of what most people experience as "normal" family life. And having been on both sides of the coin, I'm very glad my parents brought the developmentally disabled into our family. One vivid memory in particular solidified my conviction that my family's open arms and healing hearts approach was the right thing to do.

I was in junior high. Just before we had a group home, my family went to visit a large institution (now called Camp Harkness) which took care of people with special needs. It was a very austere place, with row after row of drab nondescript brick buildings. As we arrived for an event called, "Christmas in July", I felt like we were entering the movie set for *One Flew Over the Cuckoo's Nest*. A long procession of people in wheelchairs, like zombies, were carted out by orderlies and nurses, wearing drab uniforms to match the dreariness of the atmosphere.

The event was meant to be a fun day for the residents. It was anything but for me. So many of the people, I now understand, didn't need to be institutionalized, but they were, because I guess that was what society did back then. They were treated like inmates. And in many ways, they embodied what I think of when I consider how prisoners live. The residents who could walk just shuffled around, hunched over, head hanging down, with no energy or life or joy.

The nurses and staff brought out presents to all the residents. We sang songs and gave it our best effort to bring some fun to the place. Our efforts were like throwing a cup of water on a thousand-acre brush fire. The place was a fortress of sorrow.

Even though it was meant to be a celebration, I couldn't help but think, *what is every other day like?*

If this was a special day, I couldn't imagine the rest of the year. I remember what motivated the residents the most was food. More than anything else, like animals, they responded to food. It was so sad, so empty; so anti-human.

We left that day, and I struggled to reconcile what I'd seen. The diminishment of humanity was the hardest part. After we opened our home, I saw it manifest time and again with the adults who came to us. As opposed to the children, who hadn't been institutionalized for decades, the adults never broke free from the effect of being penned up their entire life. Their existence with us, for the most part, revolved around food and just passing time. It was so tragic to see the destruction of the human soul.

But, where there is despair, hope is stronger. Where there is brokenness, new life springs up. And my experience and friendship with the younger people with special needs only cemented my belief that there is nothing greater than genuine human relationship to bring healing and inspiration to another person, regardless of their mental or physical limitations.

The young people enjoyed life. They sang, they played sports. They danced, they cried, they hugged freely. In short, they lived. They had a *life*. I am so grateful to my parents, and so are dozens (maybe hundreds) of people, because they chose to do something simple, though not easy. They chose to love the unloved.

11

True Community

THIS BOOK WAS WRITTEN to encourage you. It was written to provide you with the hope that, in spite of the tragedies of this fallen world, God gives joy. He gives peace. He gives grace. And, if we say yes to Him, we get to be a part of all that He does. We don't have to say yes, however. God has given us free will. We have options. We can say "maybe" or even "no." Saying "maybe" is our way of telling Him, "Let me think about it, God." Saying "no" tells God we know best.

But, if we say yes to His commands, we get to be the "hands and feet" of Jesus. Nothing in this life can compare to the power of God working through us. Nothing can compare to the joy of seeing a life redeemed by His grace. And, when we say yes to Him, we get to be intimately involved in His redemptive work.

1 Corinthians 12:12-31 gives us a true picture of what happens when we say yes to God. This passage describes us as each being a part of the Body of Christ. Our role starts with obedience. It begins when we say yes to where He's placed us, how He's gifted us, and how He uses us to accomplish His plans. If we collectively say yes to God, I believe we will be the true community that is meant to be the Body of Christ. When we collectively say yes, the power of God makes itself known to the world.

This is the final chapter, so it's going to be my "parting shot" (for this book, anyway).

Since it's the last impression I get to make, I have included the entire passage from 1 Corinthians, Chapter 12. Over the past year, I have spent hundreds of hours in reflection as I have earnestly pursued the right words for these pages. I want my life to be a reflection of God's goodness. My deep desire is that you experience His grace for your every need. My sincere hope is that this book brings encouragement to you and the Body of

Christ. But most of all, I pray that you (and all believers) fully say yes to God.

So, without further ado, here is the passage, with my thoughts interspersed. These verses are important because they give us a picture of God's desire for our lives, and how we can be most effective in rescuing others. Note its description of how we are to interact with one another, and how we are to follow the direction of God.

> [12] For as the body is one and has many members, but all the members of that one body, being many, are one body, so also is Christ. [13] For by one Spirit we were all baptized into one body—whether Jews or Greeks, whether slaves or free—and have all been made to drink into one Spirit. [14] For in fact the body is not one member but many.

This section emphasizes the diversity of those who believe. There are many members, each bringing a different life experience into the body. We come from different countries. We are different ethnicities. We are different genders. It uses the word "many" three times in only four verses. Clearly, the apostle Paul is reinforcing the truth that we are very different. Yet, He uses the word "one" to refer to the Body of Christ and the Holy Spirit six times. Twice as much as he mentions the diversity! We may be many, but when we are baptized by the one Spirit into the one Body, we work together as one.

> [15] If the foot should say, "Because I am not a hand, I am not of the body," is it therefore not of the body? [16] And if the ear should say, "Because I am not an eye, I am not of the body," is it therefore not of the body? [17] If the whole body were an eye, where would be the hearing? If the whole were hearing, where would be the smelling? [18] But now God has set the members, each one of them, in the body just as He pleased. [19] And if they were all one member, where would the body be?

We are in one body, but we are many. This paradox, and its consequences, are seen most every week in your local church. Some weeks, the "hand" decides to do its own thing. Or the "ear" decides not to participate in its design. As we read this section, most of us are nodding our heads. For we either have been a non-compliant body part, or we know them. Let's be honest. All of us have, at some point, been a non-compliant body part. And the trouble is, just like a physical body with non-functioning parts, the Body of Christ is limited and weakened.

As a caregiver and parent of people with non-functioning body parts, I know the limitations all too well. I don't need to reiterate it at this point in the book. All of us know people with limitations. In a handicapped person's body, it's almost always the result of a birth defect or an injury. In the Body of Christ, it's the result of unresolved conflict, or an un-surrendered will and a disobedient heart. As the final verse states, "God has set the members in the body **just as He pleased**." When we are unwilling to say yes to God, the entire body suffers.

[20] But now indeed there are many members, yet one body. [21] And the eye cannot say to the hand, "I have no need of you"; nor again the head to the feet, "I have no need of you." [22] No, much rather, those members of the body which seem to be weaker are necessary. [23] And those members of the body which we think to be less honorable, on these we bestow greater honor; and our unpresentable parts have greater modesty, [24] but our presentable parts have no need. But God composed the body, having given greater honor to that part which lacks it, [25] that there should be no schism in the body, but that the members should have the same care for one another. [26] And if one member suffers, all the members suffer with it; or if one member is honored, all the members rejoice with it.

This portion is a reminder. We are **one** body. We have to work together. We can't dismiss those who are different. We can't grow envious of other members. God put this body together, and He desires that the "members should have the same care for one another." Do you care for the other parts? Or do you think you have no need of those who are not like you. How about those members who are "weaker"?

The beauty of the body is most evident when it is healthy and whole. If something isn't working right, we go to the doctor. We pray for healing. I know all about the "unpresentable parts" failing to work. As I mentioned, I've had major surgery that removed my entire colon. Let me tell you, though you can't see it, when your colon isn't working or isn't there at all, life is not good!

When a person has part of his or her body amputated, the rest of the body compensates. The way God designed us is truly amazing. But, even in those situations, there is still stress on the parts that are compensating for the loss. They weren't designed to take on the extra responsibility for the missing limb or organ. Regardless of the limitations, though, the body comes together to make it work. As great as the compensation is, it is far better for the body to be whole and working as God originally designed.

The balance and grace of an intact body, working in one accord, is God's design. In our own physical bodies, and in the Body of Christ, God prepared every part to perform in a specific way so that the entire being would reach its full potential. Until we remove envy or arrogance from our approach to other members, we have yet to say yes to God, and the Body of Christ is rendered ineffective and incomplete. When we cheer one another, and support each other, the Body of Christ is honored and influential.

> [27] Now you are the Body of Christ, and members individually. [28] And God has appointed these in the church: first apostles, second prophets, third teachers, after that miracles, then gifts of healings, helps, administrations, varieties of tongues. [29] Are all apostles? Are all prophets? Are all teachers? Are all workers of miracles? [30] Do all have gifts of healings? Do all speak with tongues? Do all interpret? [31] But earnestly desire the best gifts. And yet I show you a more excellent way.

This chapter of 1 Corinthians concludes with a few famous sentences. It's a list of gifts and works that are designed to be active in the church. Too often, it becomes a method of classification and segregation of people within the Body of Christ. We elevate pastors and people with charismatic speaking ability and ignore those who serve in the nursery. Yet, both are necessary and blessed by God to do good work. In fact, if we had to choose, I'm guessing most churches would be more blessed by great nursery volunteers than a dynamic sermon.

I'm an ordained minister, and I'm a teacher. I speak all the time – maybe too much! So, I'm not trying to pull down the great pastors and evangelists and teachers in the Kingdom. I'm trying to pull up those who serve in the background, those who go about their work with quiet faith and patience, who say yes to God regardless of recognition. In our moments of daily obedience, when we choose to serve simply to help others rather than work to be noticed, we say yes to God. In those moments, we lay the foundation for true community.

HENRI NOUWEN was a famous theologian who taught at Yale Divinity School. He had a great influence on my life. I read his books and I was once privileged to spend a day with him when we were first considering living in community. His words have stayed with me since that day, when we sat in his living room drinking coffee and eating Danish pastries.

He said, "If you want to live in community, find ten people who are like-minded and commit to praying together one day a week, for a year." We did exactly what he suggested. And, we found that as we prayed together we were able to work together and finally give our lives to one another. It truly was one of the most remarkable years of our lives.

When Gerry and I lived in community with others nearly 40 years ago, it was because we desired nothing more than to say yes to God and to see how He would move in and through our lives.

As the years go by, community remains very important for our lives. A community of believers is important for anyone who wants to say "yes" to God. When I speak on Healing in the context of community, I am speaking from first-hand knowledge, as well as a growing understanding of what it means to be part of the Body of Christ. The community aspect is revealed within our own bodies, individually. When a part of your body is in pain, what does the rest of your body do? It reacts. Your hands reach out, your eyes focus on the area, your heart increases blood flow, sending healing blood cells to the area.

It's the same in the community that is the Body of Christ. When you are in the middle of a bad situation, it's wonderful and necessary to have the other members of the community reach out to you. When you're in the middle of a fire, and you feel the heat, it's hard to be calm. It can even be hard to pray because you become consumed with what's happening. We need one another in community to survive the fires of life.

I believe healing happens in the context of community, and rarely does healing happen without community. I saw healing happen again just recently. While we were traveling to Florida, Philip's oxygen saturation levels in his blood became terribly low. In fact, it was a true life-or-death situation. At one point, while we were in the hospital, doctors came rushing down the hall because they thought Philip was dying. They couldn't believe he was alive with such low levels. Though we've been through lots of medical emergencies, each one brings the same feelings of doubt, worry, and anxiety. But the power of community brings hope, faith, and courage.

The whole time we were in the hospital with Philip I was receiving calls and messages from places as far away as Chile, Greece, Europe, and from coast to coast in the United States. One intercessor found out and sent the following message,

"Philip get sick? Not on my watch!"

It was beautiful. It was what God intended. The Body of Christ, the true community was responding to pain and bringing healing. The Body of Christ became the calm presence we needed in our time of crisis. Miraculously, Philip recovered and returned to his usual joke-telling self in a matter of days!

I've never felt the power of community so profoundly as I did during this experience. When believers join together in prayer, the power of God moves and healing comes. It's simple. It's true. We belong in community.

THE COMMUNITY that I write about isn't just a "prayer triage unit." It's not meant to be an emergency room. It's meant to be a day-in and day-out relationship of encouragement, fellowship, correction, and inspiration. It's meant to help each of us say yes to God and it's designed to help us make the most of our lives on Earth.

Everyone needs each other. I believe every person carries a purpose and destiny to build God's Kingdom. But, **the community needs you to be You, the way God planned.** You are not meant to be someone else. Identity is tragically fluid in modern culture, and the insecurities Christians carry around create tragic results. The comparison game that Paul warned us about is being played all too often in churches all over the world. Instead of looking at others and saying, "I want her gift!", we need to look at the gifts God put in us and follow Him. Every time we have "gift envy," we fail to say yes to God. We disobey His design when we deny our gifts and desire to be someone we are not.

My prayer is that our eyes would be opened to the wisdom and revelation God gives us. My call is to help others see their giftings and to realize that "We are His workmanship, created in Christ Jesus for good works, which God prepared before Creation, that we should walk in them."[18]

We are predestined, adopted, and filled with the Holy Spirit. Why would or should we ever back down? We are meant to exercise our gifts together, to show the world the love and power of the Body of Christ. And we should never artificially limit our potential because of low self-esteem, or fears about what other people will think.

As a 70-year-old woman, I see some of my peers beginning to draw back. To look for a more relaxed pace, or to retire and do nothing much to reach people. I believe we need to live in community and help others until we are no longer able. No matter how old we are, we still have potential (particularly in today's world) to go around the world.

I was teaching a class of elderly women a few years ago and I was trying to encourage them to step out in faith. I wanted them to see how great their influence could be for God, regardless of their age. So I told them the following story:

A few years ago, there was a group of grandmothers who decided to make a calendar. They all got naked and took photos and made a calendar. It ended up becoming an international sensation. I know, it's a somewhat trivial example, but I shared it with them to remind them that age is not a limitation. If anything, it should be a propellant. While we have time and hopefully, increased wisdom, to make a difference, we should not reduce our efforts. We have Jesus Christ, we should go far beyond the influence or notoriety of a dozen naked old ladies in a calendar!

I HAVE BEEN TO MANY CHURCHES, and experienced different denominations, both here in the U.S., and in other parts of the world. What I have found is that each church has a desire to fulfill their vision. They don't all do it as they should, but the intention is there. I have learned over the years that loving them, not judging their work, is what will bring change. I do my part, and they do theirs. I work with them, not against them. I use my gifts, and they use theirs.

Together, we can build the Kingdom of God. My overwhelming desire in saying yes to God is that all Christians work together. I pray that you start by asking "what if?". What if you loved God with your whole heart, your soul, and all your mind? What if you loved your neighbor as yourself?

What if, every day, as best you could, you said "yes" to God?

As crazy as it is, that's my life so far. I have always thought that if Jesus could do so much for me He can do it for anyone. He wants to use you. He will use you. All you have to do is say yes.

Endnotes

[1]Chapter 1 – Hebrews 6:10-12

[2]Chapter 1 – http://www.biblehub.com/greek/4982.htm

[3]Chapter 2 – John 13: 1-17

[4]Chapter 2 – John 13:14-17

[5]Chapter 2 – Ephesians 5:26

[6]Chapter 3 –
http://www.macleans.ca/politics/angela-merkel-the-real-leader-of-the-free-world/

[7]Chapter 3 – http://www.newyorker.com/magazine/2014/12/01/quiet-german

[8]Chapter 3 –
http://www.macleans.ca/politics/angela-merkel-the-real-leader-of-the-free-world/

[9]Chapter 6 – http://www.digitaltrends.com/features/top-10-bad-tech-predictions/3/

[10]Chapter 7 – Kolodiejchuk, Brian. *Mother Teresa: Come Be My Light: The Private Writings of the Saint of Calcutta,* Image Publishing (2009)

[11]Chapter 7 – Lewis, C.S.
https://www.scriptureseeds.org/Christianity/EfficacyofPrayer.aspx

[12]Chapter 9 – Matthew 13:21; Mark 4:17; Acts 8:1; Acts 11:19; Acts 13:50; Romans 8:35; Galatians 5:11; Galatians 6:12 and 2 Timothy 3:12

[13]Chapter 9 – Philippians 4:7

[14]Chapter 9 – Matthew 8:28

[15]Chapter 9 – Matthew 8:24

[16]Chapter 9 – Matthew 8:25

[17]Chapter 9 – Matthew 8:26

[18]Chapter 11 – Ephesians 2:10

Author's Contact Information

To contact Barbara Lachance go to:
www.generationalsolutionsllc.com
or email:
barbara@generationalsolutionsllc.com

Made in the USA
Middletown, DE
12 March 2016